Health Rights of Older People

The book examines the health rights of older persons who are more likely potentially to face various disadvantages in terms of healthcare access and affordability, thereby impacting on health outcomes. The point of departure in the analyses is that the health security of older persons is guaranteed only if a country approaches the health of its citizens out of moral obligation, viewing health and well-being as a right rather than an entitlement. Data from five countries in the ASEAN region are analysed with the intent of highlighting the health inequalities and barriers at the societal and individual levels, on the one hand, as well as the gaps at the health and healthcare policy and programmatic levels within each country, on the other. It is also intended that the analyses of the data from the selected countries which represent different stages of development, and thus income levels, provide a useful comparative framework for policymakers in the ASEAN region.

Long Thanh Giang is Associate Professor of National Economics University, Hanoi, Senior Researcher at Institute of Social and Medical Studies (ISMS), Hanoi, and Affiliate Research Fellow of the Oxford Institute of Population Ageing, University of Oxford. His research interests include the economics of ageing and health protection for older people. He earned a PhD from National Graduate Institute for Policy Studies (GRIPS) in Tokyo.

Theresa W. Devasahayam is Associate Lecturer at Singapore University of Social Sciences (SUSS). She has provided technical expertise to various projects for United Nations' agencies and the Asian Development Bank. She has a PhD in Anthropology with a concentration in feminist studies from Syracuse University, New York, U.S.A.

Routledge-GRIPS Development Forum Studies
Edited by Kenichi Ohno and Izumi Ohno
National Graduate Institute for Policy Studies, Japan

For a full list of titles in this series, visit www.routledge.com/Routledge-GRIPS-Development-Forum-Studies/book-series/GRIPS

Health Rights of Older People

Comparative Perspectives
in Southeast Asia

Edited by Long Thanh Giang and Theresa W. Devasahayam

Routledge
Taylor & Francis Group

LONDON AND NEW YORK

First published 2018
by Routledge
2 Park Square, Milton Park, Abingdon, Oxon OX14 4RN

and by Routledge
605 Third Avenue, New York, NY 10017

First issued in paperback 2020

Routledge is an imprint of the Taylor & Francis Group, an informa business

British Library Cataloguing-in-Publication Data
A catalogue record for this book is available from the British Library

Library of Congress Cataloging-in-Publication Data
Names: Giang, Long Thanh, editor.
Title: Health rights of older people : comparative perspectives in
    Southeast Asia / edited by Long Thanh Giang and Theresa W.
    Devasahayam.
Description: Milton Park, Abingdon, Oxon ; New York, NY : Routledge,
    2018. | Series: Routledge-GRIPS development forum studies ; 6 |
    Includes bibliographical references and index.
Identifiers: LCCN 2017056919 | ISBN 9781138550469 (hbk) |
    ISBN 9781315147260 (ebk)
Subjects: LCSH: Older people—Medical care—Southeast Asia. | Right to
    health—Southeast Asia.
Classification: LCC RA564.8 .H44 2018 | DDC 362.1084/60954—dc23
LC record available at https://lccn.loc.gov/2017056919

ISBN 13: 978-0-367-50428-1 (pbk)
ISBN 13: 978-1-138-55046-9 (hbk)

Typeset in Galliard
by Apex CoVantage, LLC

Long Thanh Giang

To my old-aged parents and parents-in-law,

You have sacrificed your lives as well as your well-being to help raise my wife and me, and you taught us how health is so important for an active life. And especially to my parents, you have been a great encouragement to me to undertake research on old age issues, and it is to all of you that I want to dedicate this book.

Theresa W. Devasahayam

To my dear Grandma,

As a young girl, it was you who instilled in me the importance of an education for women, and to be happy and independent.

To my Mum, who pushed me to finish the doctoral degree, without whom I would not be where and who I am today.

I hope that I have become the woman you wanted me to be!

Contents

Figures

Tables

Contributors

Chalermpol Chamchan is Assistant Professor at the Institute for Population and Social Research (IPSR), Mahidol University, Thailand. He holds a PhD in Area Studies from Kyoto University, Japan. His recent work concentrates on population ageing, health and health systems, quality of life and happiness, and sexual and reproductive health.

Theresa W. Devasahayam is Associate Lecturer at Singapore University of Social Sciences (SUSS). Her research interests include low-skilled women, migrant workers, ageing, women and politics, and women and food security. She has provided technical expertise to various projects for United Nations' agencies and the Asian Development Bank. She has a PhD in Anthropology with a concentration in feminist studies from Syracuse University, New York, U.S.A.

Long Thanh Giang is Associate Professor of National Economics University, Hanoi, Senior Researcher at Institute of Social and Medical Studies (ISMS), Hanoi, and Affiliate Research Fellow of the Oxford Institute of Population Ageing, University of Oxford. His research interests include the economics of ageing and health protection for older people. He earned a PhD from National Graduate Institute for Policy Studies (GRIPS) in Tokyo.

Rossarin Gray is Director and Associate Professor at the Institute for Population and Social Research (IPSR), Mahidol University, Thailand. She received a PhD in Demography from the Australian National University, Australia. Her research interests include well-being and health of older people. She is the Executive Secretary of the Asian Population Association (APA).

Zamri Hassan is Senior Lecturer in the Social Work programme in the Faculty of Social Sciences, Universiti Malaysia Sarawak. He received a PhD in Health and Social Care from the University of London. His areas of specialisation are health and social care, virtual community, and community development.

How Kee Ling was formerly Associate Professor at the Faculty of Social Sciences, Universiti Malaysia Sarawak, and her teaching and research focused on disability, ageing, and women's issues. She obtained a PhD in Social Work and Social Policy from the University of Queensland, Australia. She currently serves as a consultant for UNICEF, Malaysia.

Faizah Mas'ud is Senior Lecturer of Faculty of Social Sciences, Universiti Malaysia Sarawak. She completed her doctoral degree in social work from the University of Western Australia. Her research interests include social work and social policy issues, in particular disability, family, and child welfare.

Tham Hong Thi Pham is Lecturer of the Faculty of Mathematical Economics at the National Economics University. She is completing her PhD dissertation on costing healthcare services for older people in Vietnam. Her main research interests are cost analysis and actuarial projections of healthcare services.

Phong Manh Phi is Lecturer of the Department of Political Theories, University of Mining and Geology, Hanoi. His main research interests are health insurance and anti-poverty policies for older people in Vietnam. He is now completing his doctoral work on these issues at the Vietnam National University.

S. Irudaya Rajan is Professor at the Centre for Development Studies, Thiruvananthapuram, Kerala. He is the President of the Association of Gerontology (AGI) as well as Kerala Economic Association (KEA). He has research experience in social, economic, health, and demographic facets of population ageing.

Sidiah John Siop is Head of the Nursing Department, Faculty of Medicine and Health Sciences, Universiti Malaysia Sarawak. She obtained her PhD in Gerontology from Universiti Putra Malaysia. She has served in several health districts in Sarawak. Her research interests include disability, quality of life, and health needs of older people.

Kusol Soonthorndhada was Associate Professor at the Institute for Population and Social Research (IPSR), Mahidol University from 1990 to 2016. She obtained a PhD in Population and Development from the National Institute of Development Administration, Thailand. Her research focuses on population ageing and health.

Sreerupa is a guest faculty member at the School of Human Studies, Ambedkar University Delhi, India. She received a PhD in Economics from the Jawaharlal Nehru University. Her broad research interest includes population ageing, with a concentration on gender, health, healthcare, and care work.

Hein Thet Ssoe is a medical doctor and has a bachelor's degree in medicine and surgery from the University of Medicine, Myanmar. He is now a health and nutrition coordinator for the HelpAge International, Myanmar and leads programmes on healthcare, home care, and nutrition intervention for vulnerable older people in rural communities.

Foreword

Not long ago in our memory, Southeast Asia was a region of Flying Geese whose young and vigorous population produced high economic growth rates, shrinking poverty levels, and rapid urbanization and structural transformations. There has been rich research examining these trends from a variety of perspectives—social, political or economic. Several decades later, the region faces new and more challenging problems generated precisely because its countries have succeeded in attaining high economic and income growth rates, resulting in demographic changes. Social scientists are now taking on the task of explaining how this situation has come about but, more importantly, investigating and providing useful insights needed to guide policymakers to address effectively these new challenges. Dr. Giang Thanh Long, a co-editor of this book, is a long-time friend of mine and was one of the original staff of the Vietnam Development Forum, a policy research unit which I founded in Hanoi in 2004. He and his colleagues have picked an emerging issue and written just the right book for national leaders and ministries tasked to improve the welfare of ageing populations. This book is unique in that it focuses on a significant topic of interest to not only scholars but policymakers—the rights of older persons in the context of health. The book is a compilation of studies on the health rights of older persons in five countries in Southeast Asia. Each chapter seeks to answer a question by using a common analytical framework. This has imparted concreteness, comparability and technical precision to their joint work. In fact, the systematic collection and comparison of successful and not-so-successful international experiences is a highly commendable method for extracting practical policy knowledge. It is hoped that policy practitioners and researchers will gain much from this book and that similar research endeavours for other demographic challenges generated by high economic growth rates in Southeast Asia as well as in other developing regions of the world will be undertaken.

Kenichi Ohno
Professor
National Graduate Institute for Policy Studies

Preface

According to human rights theory, a person has the same rights as every other person because of the very fact of being human. Human rights are a fundamental part of life, as it protects basic human needs and demands by recognising our freedom to make life choices and develop our potential as human beings. Because we live in a diverse world which is marked by increasing complexity, the protection of rights is ever more important to promote justice and equality, on the one hand, and to reduce tyranny, on the other. In reality, however, a diverse world presupposes social hierarchies lending to the marginalisation of some groups of persons over others and, in turn, the violation of those groups' rights. Older persons, for example, are a good example of an increasingly marginalised group. Protecting their rights as humans as a collective would also entail protecting their health rights.

This book represents an attempt in the study of the health rights of older persons from five countries in the ASEAN. As editors who spearheaded this study, our aim was to say something distinctive about the health of older people while providing an introduction to the debate on rights, and in this case the health rights of older people, suggesting what might be done to resolve a particular set of challenges and problems facing a growing group of persons today. A study never attempted before among countries in the ASEAN, the editors of this volume not only saw value in pursuing the topic as population ageing sweeps through the countries in the region, but also because it is an under-researched area.

As editors, we want to acknowledge the Institute of Human Rights and Peace Studies at Mahidol University without which we would not have been able to conduct this research project on health rights and older persons through a grant from the SHAPE-SEA program supported by the Swedish International Development Cooperation Agency (SIDA) and the Norwegian Centre for Human Rights (NCHR). In particular, we wish to extend our gratitude to Dr. Naparat Kranrattanasuit, Advisor of SHAPE-SEA, for her support and guidance. We also would like to thank Joel Mark Barredo for his timely administrative support.

We are grateful to Professor Kenichi Ohno of the National Graduate Institute for Policy Studies (GRIPS) in Tokyo for encouraging us to publish this book as a volume in the Routledge-GRIPS Development Forum Studies. We are also thankful to Yongling Lam and Samantha Phua for their enthusiastic support in assisting us in producing this book.

On behalf of the authors, we would like to thank the various organisations and local authorities in all the five countries who have helped us in one way or other in the collection of data for this book. A big thank you also goes to all the older persons who were willing to participate in the study conducted in the respective countries.

Last but not least, we would also like to thank the chapter contributors who have made this book possible. We have learned much from each other in this journey, and our hope is that this volume will be a useful compendium not only to policymakers and NGO practitioners working in the area of ageing in the ASEAN region but also to academics pursuing work in the area of health among older people.

Long Thanh Giang and Theresa W. Devasahayam

Abbreviations

ADL	Activities of Daily Living
A&E	Accident & Emergency
AIC	The Agency for Integrated Care (Singapore)
ASEAN	Association for Southeast Asian Nations
BHS	Basic Healthcare Sum (Singapore)
BHS	Basic Health Staff (Myanmar)
CAI	Committee on Ageing Issues (Singapore)
CDMP	Chronic Disease Management Programme (Singapore)
CHAS	Community Health Assist Scheme (Singapore)
CMU	Chiangmai University (Thailand)
COPD	Chronic Obstructive Pulmonary Disease
CPF	Central Provident Fund (Singapore)
CSC	Civil Service Card (Singapore)
CSMBS	Civil Servant Medical Benefit Scheme (Thailand)
DHS	District Health System
DM	Diabetes Mellitus
FGD	Focus Group Discussion
FP	Family Physician
GDP	Gross Domestic Product
GP	General Practitioner
GSO	General Statistics Office (Vietnam)
HAI	HelpAge International
HDB	Housing and Development Board (Singapore)
IDI	In-Depth Interview
IMC	Inter-Ministerial Committee on the Ageing Population (Singapore)
IMCHCE	Inter-Ministerial Committee on Health Care for the Elderly (Singapore)
LGO	Local Government Organisation (Thailand)
LTC	Long-term Care
MCA	Ministerial Committee on Ageing (Singapore)
MMS	Medisave Minimum Sum (Singapore)
MOH	Ministry of Health

MOHH MOH Holdings (Singapore)
MOHS Ministry of Health and Sports (Myanmar)
MOPH Ministry of Public Health
MSF Ministry of Social and Family Development (Singapore)
NACFA National Advisory Council on the Family and the Aged (Singapore)
NCDs Non-Communicable Diseases
NGO Non-Governmental Organization
NHSO National Health Security Office (Thailand)
NPE National Policy for the Elderly (Malaysia)
NSO National Statistics Office (Thailand)
OECD Organisation for Economic Co-operation and Development
OOP Out-Of-Pocket
PGP Pioneer Generation Package (Singapore)
PHC Primary Health Centre (Myanmar)
PP Health promotion and disease prevention (Thailand)
PSU Primary Sampling Unit
Q1-Q5 Income quintile (20 percent poorest – 20 percent richest)
RHC Rural Health Centre (Myanmar)
RRA Retirement and Re-employment Act (Singapore)
SHI Social Health Insurance (Vietnam)
SHPH Sub-district Health Promotion Hospitals (Thailand)
SRHC Sub-Rural Health Centre (Malaysia and Myanmar)
SSS Social Security Scheme (Thailand)
UHCS Universal Health Coverage Scheme (Thailand)
UN United Nations
UNFPA United Nations Population Fund
VAE Vietnam Association of the Elderly (Vietnam)
VNCA Vietnam National Committee on Ageing
VWOs Voluntary Welfare Organisation (Singapore)
WHO World Health Organization

1 Ageing and health in Southeast Asia

Theresa W. Devasahayam and Long Thanh Giang

1.1 Introduction

The last century has seen an ageing tsunami as never seen before. Populations across the world have been ageing at an unprecedented pace. Population ageing, defined as an increase in the proportion of older persons (OPs) in the population aged 60 years and more, is an emerging reality for many countries. Felt initially in the developed countries, population ageing has been seen as the dominant characteristic of demographic change in the developing countries since the later part of the last century. In fact, developing countries are ageing far more rapidly than the more developed countries as a result of faster declines in fertility (Gist and Velkoff 1997) and improvements in longevity (United Nations Population Fund and HelpAge International 2012). According to the Department of Economic and Social Affairs, Population Division (2015), currently one in eight people worldwide is aged 60 years or over, and it is expected that the numbers will increase to one in six persons by 2030. World population estimates show that in 2030, the percentage of OPs is projected to increase to 16.5 percent from the current 12.3 percent.

As much as the rest of the world has been ageing, Asia has shown similar demographic trends. Currently, around 60 percent of the world's elderly are from Asia and the Pacific region (Economic and Social Commission for Asia and the Pacific 2017). In 2016, 12.4 percent of a total population of 4,454 million in this region was 60 and above. By 2030, 17 percent of Asia's population will be ageing (Department of Economic and Social Affairs, Population Division 2015). In fact, from 2016 to 2050, the number of OPs in the region is expected to be more than double from 547 million to 1.3 billion (Economic and Social Commission for Asia and the Pacific 2017), with the elderly aged 60 and above projected to constitute 20.1 percent of a total population of 5,169 million. In other words, it has been projected that in 2050 one in four people are expected to be 60 years and above while the proportion of the "oldest-old", that is, those in the 80+ cohort, is expected to comprise one-fifth of the elderly population.

Among the ASEAN countries, the trends are similar: in 2016, 9.6 percent of the region's total population of 640 million was 60 and above and in 2050, the older

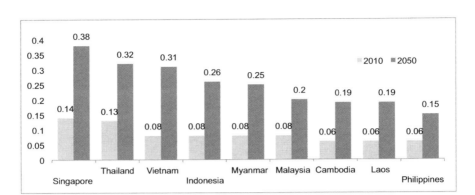

Figure 1.1 Percentage of older population in ASEAN countries, 2010 and 2050
Source: UN Population Division World Population Prospects: The 2010 Revision (Medium Fertility Variant)

population is expected to be 21.1 percent, respectively. While the speed at which ageing is taking place in the countries in Southeast Asia has been recorded at 23 percent, this is far less than the countries in the Pacific region which was the highest in the Asia Pacific recorded at 74 percent (Economic and Social Commission for Asia and the Pacific Population Data Sheet 2016). Singapore records the highest proportion of persons aged 60 and above at 14 percent in 2010, while Thailand's proportion of 60 and above stands at 13 percent (Figure 1.1). Following are Vietnam (10.7 percent), Indonesia (8.5 percent), Malaysia (7.8 percent) and Myanmar (6.7 percent), while the proportion of 60 and above in Cambodia, Laos and the Philippines records at 6 percent. Translated in life expectancy terms, an older population suggests an increase in life expectancy at birth.

Following the global demographic trends, a feminisation of ageing characterised by a higher proportion of women than men in the old age cohorts has been observed in the ASEAN (Association for Southeast Asian Nations) countries (Table 1.1). The proportion of older women increases with increasing age. In Singapore, for example, there were 200 women aged 60 and older for every 100 men in 2016 (Department of Statistics 2016). Among those aged 80 and above, there were 165 women for every 100 men.

By gender, women of Singapore enjoy a life expectancy of 86.4 years followed by women from Brunei Darussalam at 81.1 years, according to 2016 ESCAP (Economic and Social Commission for the Asia and Pacific) figures. In third spot for female life expectancy is that of Vietnam at 80.7 years, while Thailand is ranked fourth at 78.2 years, followed by Malaysia at 77.4 years. Next are the Philippines at 72.1 years, Indonesia at 71.4 years and Cambodia at 71.2 years, respectively (Table 1.2).

Table 1.1 Feminisation of ageing in Southeast Asian countries, 1950–2050

Country	Percentage of females in older population					Percentage of females in the oldest old population				
	1950	1975	2000	2025	2050	1950	1975	2000	2025	2050
Cambodia	54.7	54.6	65.1	59.8	56.1	58.2	60.3	59.3	67.9	66.5
Indonesia	51.5	53.4	54.2	53.55	54.5	53.5	58.2	54.2	53.5	54.5
Laos	53.5	52.3	53.2	53.55	52.3	60.0	58.5	55.9	58.6	57.1
Malaysia	47.7	49.6	52.7	54.05	54.2	50.1	54.9	56.7	62.1	63.9
Myanmar	54.9	58.3	53.5	54.85	55.1	62.0	56.8	56.9	58.8	60.9
Philippines	61.8	54.1	54.6	54.05	54.3	66.2	66.2	61.9	60.9	64.4
Singapore	60.0	52.2	53.5	53.15	54.3	64.3	65.6	61.6	60.1	60.7
Thailand	55.5	54.1	54.7	55.45	55.9	60.7	60.7	60.6	65.2	65.4
Timor-Leste	55.7	51.8	50.8	52.75	50.8	60.0	61.5	59.5	55.8	57.5
Vietnam	55.0	54.0	53.3	53.35	53.8	62.0	60.2	57.3	58.0	60.5

Source: Adapted from Mujahid (2006)

Table 1.2 Life expectancy for countries in Southeast Asia, by gender

Countries	Life expectancy	
	Male	Female
Brunei Darussalam	77.5	81.1
Cambodia	67.1	71.2
Indonesia	67.2	71.4
Lao PDR	65.6	68.4
Malaysia	72.7	77.4
Myanmar	64.2	68.3
Philippines	65.2	72.1
Singapore	80.3	86.4
Thailand	71.5	78.2
Timor-Leste	67.1	70.7
Vietnam	71.4	80.7

Source: Economic and Social Commission for Asia and the Pacific (2016)

Relative to global rankings, however, Singapore, in particular, has done comparably well in terms of life expectancy: it took the sixth spot for males and ninth for females (Ministry of Health 2016). Moreover, women are more likely to experience widowhood compared to men since women tend to marry older men, in keeping with social and cultural norms.

As in the rest of the world, the twin drivers for population ageing in the countries in Southeast Asia have been falling fertility levels and rising life expectancy. The latter characterised by a rise in the proportion of OPs stems from enhanced healthcare services, medical technologies, and to some extent, better nutrition. Data collected over 29 years (1980–2008) from Cambodia, Laos and Myanmar showed that socioeconomic status and healthcare resources were critical in the rise in life expectancy (Chan and Taylor 2012). Increasing educational levels was also a significant factor for a shift in the demographic transition (Jones 2013). In a growing educated population, individuals are more inclined to adopt healthy lifestyles compared with past generations.

On the downside, an ageing population means that the dependency ratio increases, placing a greater burden on the working population as well as on the healthcare system of the respective countries in the region. There is a complex and dynamic relationship between health and ageing. OPs have different health-care requirements because of the growing burden of chronic illnesses, injuries and disabilities and increasing concerns about future caregiving, and thus health-care systems will need to adapt in order to provide adequate care to this age cohort (cf. Lehnert et al. 2011; Bähler, Huber, Brüngger and Reich 2015). However, the increasing burden of healthcare expenditures is largely a policy and cost management concern rather than a demographic one (Getzen 1992). As Sarah Harper (2013: 22) maintains: "the predicted increases in medical and health care costs are not as a result of growing numbers of older people *per se*, but as a result of *current policy frameworks* within which these costs will occur". A growing proportion of OPs undoubtedly means an increase in healthcare needs and costs since OPs are more likely to have health issues (Garrett and Martini 2007; Kespichayawattana and Jitapunkul 2009; Doubova et al. 2015). In fact, the roles and resources of the state and corporate enterprises respectively have had immense consequences on a society's needs as well as its access to healthcare (Estes and Linkins 2007). While access to healthcare is a major determinant of health outcomes, social and environmental factors are equally significant in directly affecting health status and, in turn, the life expectancy of individuals.

Because OPs place higher demands on pension, healthcare and social benefit programmes thereby impacting on the fiscal and macroeconomic stability in many countries, population ageing presents a concern to governments (National Research Council 2012; Mujahid 2006). Because of these concerns, the ageing population has come to be called the 'demographic time bomb', spurring governments to put in place policies to avert the dire economic consequences a growing old age population could have on the country's resources. However, the burden of ageing has been regarded to be greater for developing countries that are undergoing ageing because of having fewer resources compared to the affluent economies (Gerst-Emerson, Wong, Michaels-Obregon and Palloni 2015).

There has been explicit concern with older women's vulnerabilities in the economic, health and social fronts, a point which was highlighted in the Plan of Action adopted by the Second World Assembly on Ageing in Madrid in 2002, since older women have been considered to face greater disadvantages in older age compared to older men given their accumulated vulnerabilities throughout the life course (cf. Devasahayam 2014). In this regard, concerns of governments have also been spurred by the steady growth of older women among the ageing population. The proportion of older women vis-à-vis the larger population has gradually inched its way up over the last fifty years, a trend which will continue into 2050, as captured in the above table.

1.2   Health, older persons' and human rights: how they matter

Worldwide, the rise in life expectancy in the 20th century has been attributed to advancements in medical technologies coupled with other determinants of health such as growing levels of education and income levels matched with improved public health measures (Bunker 2001). The evolution of medical technologies and more aggressive treatment protocols have reduced mortality related to cardiovascular and cerebrovascular diseases (Fuchs 2011; Mackenbach 1996). In the last fifty years, medical technologies have changed the practice of medicine, saved lives and increased access to care. Medical technologies have resulted in improved quality of life as people are able to live healthier, more productive and independent lives because of leading normal or close to normal lives. Recent decades have also seen innovations in medical technology that have become an important driver for delivering efficiencies in healthcare systems such that now hospital stays have shortened significantly. Although sophisticated medical technology is already available in developed countries, the landscape is constantly changing, with further advances made each year with the introduction of new treatments.

Although medical advancements have played a significant role in bringing about benefits in reducing mortality and extending life expectancy, advances in medical technologies have raised concerns about rising medical and healthcare costs, especially among the elderly (Cutler, Rosen and Vijan 2006; cf. Kumar 2011). Because of spiralling healthcare costs and the difficulties OPs may encounter in accessing healthcare in some countries, there have been arguments put forth for their health rights. Following Farmer (1999: 1487), health and access to appropriate medical care are bound up with social and economic rights and "are every bit as critical as civil rights" (Farmer 1999: 1487).

Much has been written about the human rights discourse and how human right norms have been received, applied and adapted in different contexts (Donnelly 2003; Clapham 2006; Hafner-Burton and Tsutsui 2005; Risse and Sikkink 1999). Across the world, there are numerous examples of how global human rights norms have influenced national government practices (Shahid and Yerbury 2014; Donnelly and Whelan 2017). In recent decades, the world has seen the emergence of various organisations and groups aimed at tracking rights violations (Simmons 2009). In the evolution of human rights, the world has also seen how the concept has become applied to various groups from the child and woman to the migrant (Brownlie and Goodwin-Gill 2010).

Because of the growing older population across the world, there has been a push from different quarters for the development of a rights convention related to the protection of OPs, citing the lack of a legal gap addressing concerns and interests of this group (Doron and Apter 2010). Some have argued that the time is ripe for the promulgation of an international Convention on the Rights of Older Persons because of changing demographics around the world and the lack of a binding international instrument that addresses the rights of OPs. Moreover, arguments have been made that a convention is necessary because it is an effective legal tool for social protection. Currently, while the rights of OPs may be protected under some conventions, the concern is that "older people experience specific forms of rights violation based on their age" (Fredvang and Biggs 2012: 15) and there is not "sufficient attention either in the wording of existing human rights instruments or in the practice of human rights bodies and mechanisms" granted to OPs, as the Human Rights Council discovered in a 2013 consultation (Ryan 2014).

While seeing the value of the concept of elder rights because of rapidly ageing societies, the book selectively examines the health rights of OPs – a concept that the authors have chosen to focus on given that increasing age brings on an increasing need for healthcare services. Farmer (2003) maintains that health rights is integral to the well-being of an OP especially since it deals with the most basic right – the right to survival. By health rights, the authors mean freedoms safeguarded by the state to access appropriate and relevant healthcare and health information at any time (cf. Farmer 2003) coupled with the right to a reasonable quality of life, information and privacy since for many OPs health-care services can become more unaffordable, or they may be denied timely health services because of their inability to cover the costs (Fredvang and Biggs 2012). In this case, the term 'health rights' is appropriate since it implies accessing the "highest attainable standard of health" even among those marginalised in society, such as OPs, who are more likely to face difficulties in accessing healthcare because of the lack of adequate resources in spite of needing it the most compared with other age groups (Baer, Bhushan, Taleb, Vasquez and Thomas 2016: S206). Among the elderly, the inequalities of wealth, status and power experienced also by minorities or women could be correlated to the accumulated disadvantages experienced over the life course (Estes and Linkins 2007).

The purpose of the book is to examine state rule on the realization of the rights of OPs in the area of healthcare systems and health outcomes. To put it differently, the discussion focuses on the examination of "human rights in health-relevant settings" (Mann 2006: 1940). The assumption here is that OPs are only able to exercise their health rights based on whether the healthcare system and structures enable and empower them to do so. As much as human rights has been declared as universal, the book takes a similar position in that health rights may be treated as a universal concept applicable across cultures and time. While the concept of rights to a large extent is concerned with the legalities implemented to protect OPs' entitlements (Freeman 2011), the authors of this book are more concerned with whether states act out of moral obligation to protect the health and well-being of OPs through policies and programmes. If it is from a moral and justice vantage point that states make decisions and act upon to protect the health rights of their citizenry, it follows then that robust healthcare systems and processes will be put in place so as to enable and empower the elderly and ensure that the health and well-being of each and every OP is cared for because it is a question of an individual's right. In this case, while the authors acknowledge that policies and programmes are integral to enabling the realisation of entitlements and claims to health, they assert that healthcare access and outcomes should go beyond being framed as health policy decisions or service delivery issues, requiring technical inputs or, for that matter, a product of state generosity. Following London (2008: 67), we affirm that

> the importance of recognizing the indivisibility of civil and political rights *and* socioeconomic rights means that health policymakers need to spend as much time considering and developing health policies in terms of obligations to fulfil the right to health, as they do in developing elaborate and potentially impressive commitments to eradicating discrimination or violations of dignity.

The underlying basis for choosing a rights approach in understanding health and healthcare access stems from the recognition that health inequalities exist (London 2008). In the case of OPs, they are more likely to face barriers in accessing healthcare because of the lack of resources. Health inequalities thus emerge owing to varied factors. Health inequities refer to "systematic differences in the health status of different population groups" (World Health Organization 2018a), an implication of which is that the lower the status of the individual in a society, the higher his or her risk is to having poor health outcomes. Concomitantly, those at the lower strata of society are more likely to have poorer access to appropriate, relevant and timely healthcare. In this case, social determinants such as age, gender, ethnicity/race, marital status and socioeconomic class act as critical conditions shaping an individual's access to healthcare (Albrecht, Fitzpatrick and Scrimshaw 2007), although it has been pointed out that often ethnicity/race is a proxy for socioeconomic status (LaVeist 1994; Schulman, Rubenstein, Chesley and Eisenberg 1995, as cited in Kasper 2007). For example, retirement income is appreciably less than work income, which could impact on access to healthcare. Moreover, access to healthcare has been suggested as being synonymous to barriers to healthcare. Such barriers include poverty and socioeconomic differences, culture and psychosocial factors, impacting on service use (Kasper 2007).

In a nutshell, a health rights approach embraces a "realization of health for all . . . based on social justice", entailing the workings of the state to overcome social and economic inequalities through health policies and programmes to protect the dignity of the person (London 2008: 66). In the area of health, we can say that the rights violations of OPs to appropriate, timely and relevant healthcare services are "deeper pathologies of power" related to abuse or assaults on their dignity (Farmer 2003: 7). These offences against the dignity of OPs may be intersected and thereby compounded by a range of discriminations based on poverty, racism and gender inequality (Farmer 2003). In this case, promoting and protecting the health of the OP is dependent upon the promotion and protection of the rights and dignity of the elderly as a whole. Thus the focal point of analysis is the "whole human being made vulnerable to a wide variety of pathogens and unhealthy conditions as a result of how the person is treated by society" (Mann 2006: 1940).

1.3   Rationale for the book

The bulk of theoretical and policy research on population ageing has focused on the disadvantages OPs have experienced on different fronts – economic, social and health contexts. The disadvantages faced by OPs range from declining informal family support, increasing longevity and widespread poverty. Various risk factors, such as lack of access to regular income and work, adequate healthcare services, and increasing dependency are determinants of old-age poverty and have also become salient concerns of OPs. In this case, OPs are a vulnerable group as they tend to have fewer savings and are less healthy than younger people and as a result might be either denied medical treatment or might end up receiving poorer or insufficient healthcare. Moreover, OPs may face various kinds of stigmatisation and discrimination often based on misconceptions, stereotypes and fears about OPs being a burden to society. One argument is that the vulnerabilities faced by OPs are brought on because they are forced to transfer their roles and responsibilities to the younger generation as a result of being perceived as disruptive to the social order. In this case, the assumption is that OPs and children are less productive than middle-aged persons and, therefore, are stereotyped as being 'second-class citizens' (Henkens 2005; Posthuma and Campion 2009). Because OPs have less status and power, they are also more vulnerable to social deprivation and poverty. But since OPs have the greatest potential to compete with the younger generation for resources, it has been argued that limits on their resource consumption may be the only viable alternative to help other vulnerable groups in society (Callahan 1987), thereby leading to their own marginalisation.

Because OPs potentially face various disadvantages, there is greater reason to ensure their rights or security as a group is protected. One area in which their rights may not be protected is in health security, a theme that is taken up for discussion in this book. The primary objective is to examine if the concept of health rights of OPs and, in turn, their health security have been integrated into the formulation of health and healthcare policies targeted at older people in five ASEAN countries (i.e., Singapore, Malaysia, Thailand, Vietnam and Myanmar), which have diverse socioeconomic and health indicators (Table 1.3). Owing to the accelerated rate at which ASEAN countries are undergoing population ageing, the number of older people who will be left behind and, in turn, experience discrimination and violation of rights is likely to increase. In the case of health rights among them, older people may not receive appropriate health and social care because of discriminatory practices held against them because of their age. Treatments can be withheld from them and older people may end up receiving

Table 1.3 Socioeconomic and health indicators of five studied countries, 2014

	Singapore	*Malaysia*	*Thailand*	*Vietnam*	*Myanmar*
Total population (mil. persons)	5.47	29.9	67.7	90.7	53.4
Population growth rate (percent)	1.30	1.47	0.41	1.07	0.85
Fertility rate	1.25	1.94	1.51	1.96	2.20
Proportion of elderly aged 65+ (percent)	11.05	5.67	10.1	6.62	5.24
Life expectancy at birth	82.5	74.7	74.4	75.6	65.9
GDP per capita (constant 2011 international $)	80,192	23,646	14,976	5,106	4,635
Health expenditure as percent GDP	4.92	4.17	4.12	7.07	2.28
Health expenditure per capita, PPP (constant 2011 international $)	4,047	1,040	600	390	103

Source: Own compilations from World Bank (2017).

poor or insufficient health services. In this case, the discussion in this book is critical for increasing an understanding of the extent to which older people's rights are protected and why it is imperative to address the fundamental cause of discrimination and the violation of rights in the area of health security.

While greater focus has been granted to the analysis of policy formulation and implementation informed by research on ageing, this book seeks to understand health security from the point of view of OPs for several reasons. First, the onset of ageing is linked to a greater use of healthcare services, and an understanding of health security will provide a lens into the extent to which OPs' rights are protected in a country. Second, OPs may not receive adequate healthcare because governments may be facing other more pressing issues or may not have sufficient resources to address the increasing needs of a growing older population. Third, exploring the experiences of the health security of OPs from an ASEAN perspective will enable the emergence of valuable lessons for different countries at different income levels on how each promotes health security among OPs in the respective countries and in the ASEAN region as a whole.

In the ASEAN region, many governments continue to view ageing predominantly as a social welfare or development issue rather than view the needs of OPs within a rights framework. Because of this, the likelihood of OPs becoming recipients of charity rather than individuals who should be enjoying equal rights as every other citizen in the country tends to be the norm. A paradigm shift, thus, is needed for countries to move from a social welfare- to a rights-based approach to ensure the rights of OPs. In addition, national standards on the rights of OPs tend to be patchy and inconsistent in countries across the world. As a result, few countries collect data on violations of the rights of OPs. For this reason, among others, violations will continue unaddressed as long as there is a lack of information on the nature, prevalence and causes of rights abuses faced by OPs. Thus, the ensuing discussion in the following chapters intends to provide a framework to guide policy decision-makers to ensure that OPs have access to health and social security, to allocate the country's resources fairly to promote equality, and to improve the quality of health and social care that will lead to improved health outcomes, including promote age-sensitive programmes in healthcare in order that recipients of aged care services are treated with respect and dignity.

1.4   Understanding 'health rights' and framing analyses in this book

1.4.1   How health rights are measured

According to the World Health Organization (2017), the goal of the human rights-based approach is to ensure that all health policies, strategies and programmes are designed with the objective of improving individual's right to health. Health rights may be measured according to the following principles and standards:

- **Non-discrimination** which seeks "to guarantee that human rights are exercised without discrimination of any kind based on race, colour, sex, language, religion, political or other opinion, national or social origin, property, birth or other status such as disability, age, marital and family status, sexual orientation and gender identity, health status, place of residence, economic and social situation" (World Health Organization 2017)
- **Availability** in that "a sufficient quantity of functioning public health and health care facilities, goods and services, as well as programs" (Baer et al. 2016: S209). Among OPs, this refers to the extent of availability of health services, facilities and tools to meet the health needs of OPs. In terms of medicines, this implies that OPs are ensured that the essential medicines they require are available as part of the "core minimum obligations under the right to health" (Baer et al. 2016: S209). The availability of pain-relieving medicines is also integral to palliative and end-of-life care, increasingly being framed as a critical human rights issue linked to human dignity and human rights (Morrissey, Herr and Levine 2015, as cited in Baer et al. 2016). In many countries, the availability of pain-relieving medicines has been considered controlled substances and therefore their supply and

distribution have been restricted when needed. Moreover, availability may also refer to whether there is an adequate supply of physicians, dentists and other providers; of facilities such as clinics and hospitals; and of specialised programmes and services such as geriatric, mental health and emergency care (Penchansky and Thomas 1981).

- **Accessibility** in that health facilities, goods and services are accessible to everyone. This point has four overlapping dimensions: (a) non-discrimination, (b) physical accessibility, (c) economical accessibility (affordability) and (d) information accessibility.

    In terms of direct non-discrimination, OPs are deliberately excluded from accessing services because of their age. In keeping with the Sustainable Development Goal (SDG) 3 that reiterates health "for all at all ages", health promotion and disease prevention programmes and activities should be designed to meet the needs of all age groups, both young and old (World Health Organization 2018b). Specifically, health promotion and disease prevention programmes and activities should meet the needs of older people, who might have particular needs related to functional and cognitive decline (Baer et al. 2016). Non-discrimination starts at the policy level, which ensures that older people's needs are taken into account. Older people should also not be neglected in the dissemination of health information. Ensuring a right to health also entails physical accessibility taking into account the location of supply and location of clients (Penchansky and Thomas 1981). This refers to the built environment and dimensions, such as distance to health facilities, availability of transport and the walkability of neighbourhoods. Physical accessibility also entails that the health facilities are in safe reach without posing unacceptable risks to the life and health of the elderly person (Baer et al. 2016). The provision of adequate transportation in this regard improves accessibility. Moreover, ensuring health rights is bound up with accessing health information. Accessibility, in fact, includes "the right to seek, receive, and impart health-related information in an accessible format" (Baer et al. 2016: S211). The assumption here is that health information is a human right as well as an underlying determinant of health. Because literacy rates tend to be lower among OPs, realising the health rights of the OPs would entail interventions that focus on improving literacy among OPs.

- **Affordability** which is crucial in accessing healthcare services and realising one's health rights. This involves prices of services, providers' insurance, or deposit requirements in relation to the clients' income, ability to pay and existing health insurance (Penchansky and Thomas 1981). In many countries, OPs have fewer resources than younger people, especially if they were to be living off their savings. In low- and middle-income countries, OPs are financially vulnerable since social security systems tend to be weak (Baer et al. 2016). Certain groups within the elderly population are particularly vulnerable such as older women who are unable to pay the premiums for health insurance and, therefore, are not adequately covered.

- **Acceptability** which suggests that all health facilities, goods and services must be culturally appropriate as well as sensitive to specific groups of people. This includes whether "services are age friendly or responsive to older people's needs, taking into account the diversity of older people, as they are not a homogeneous group but face varying health risks and circumstances" (Baer et al. 2016: S211). In particular, healthcare services would be considered to fulfil the criterion of acceptability if they met the needs of specific groups of OPs such as those living with disabilities, living in extreme poverty, or are from minority ethnic groups or groups with certain sexual orientations such as lesbian, gay, bisexual and transgender communities, or come from ethnic minorities, refugee and displaced populations.
- **Adequacy/Appropriateness (or Quality of Services)** in that all health facilities, goods and services must be scientifically and medically appropriate and of good quality. The quality of health services also includes adequately skilled, competent and empathetic healthcare workers who play a critical role in assuring good-quality health services to the elderly. Among healthcare practitioners, there should be a good mix of specialists, as well as an adequate supply of geriatricians.

1.4.2   Framing analyses of health rights in country case studies

Since the aim of the study was to uncover the health rights paradigm, specifically in respect to accessibility and adequacy of healthcare provisions in each of the five countries selected in the ASEAN, it was determined that both primary and secondary research approaches would be necessary.

Primary data collection involved gathering qualitative data in the different countries through in-depth interviews (IDIs) and focus group discussions (FGDs) to yield qualitative data. In all the five countries, qualitative data was collected through the use of a standardised interview schedule. The survey tools included a list of open-ended questions aimed at uncovering how OPs access healthcare and the types of obstacles they might encounter. The topics and questions covered in the qualitative data collection component of the research are tabulated below (Table 1.4). In all the countries, IDIs were also conducted with NGOs working on eldercare or ageing issues. In some countries, local government officials and local authorities, as well as healthcare providers were also interviewed. It is worth noting that the topics and questions in Table 1.4 provided general guidelines for the country research teams to collect data. In each country, questions were modified to adapt with socioeconomic and cultural contexts.

Only in two countries (Malaysia and Singapore) were the survey questionnaires distributed with the aim of collecting quantitative data. The quantitative data were collected via the distribution of the survey questionnaire entitled "Health Security of Older Persons" which was originally produced by HelpAge International (HAI) for Myanmar. For the purposes of distribution in Singapore and Malaysia, the original questionnaire, however, was modified to fit the Malaysia and Singapore contexts. A quantitative survey questionnaire was distributed because of the lack of national surveys. The quantitative survey covered different

Table 1.4 Topics covered in the qualitative surveys

1. **General /recent experiences**
   - Could you describe the experiences you have had in using the services provided by the health centres/ private clinics/ government hospitals/ private hospitals?
   - Could you rate the care and attention you have received from the healthcare professionals/workers/staff at the healthcare facility?
   - How satisfied were you in your recent visit(s) to the healthcare facility or provider?

2. **Accessibility/availability of health facilities**
   - Which is the nearest healthcare facility or provider to you?
   - Would you say that the healthcare facility or provider is relatively accessible to you?
   - How far do you have to travel (distance/time/other factors) to reach this healthcare facility?

3. **Affordability**
   - Does the cost of treatment affect your decision to access healthcare?
   - Could you tell us why and in what ways does affordability affect the treatment choices you make?
   - Do you think the government adequately covers your healthcare costs? If not, why?

4. **Appropriateness/satisfaction on healthcare facility**
   - Which healthcare facility or providers do you have the most trust in? Why?
   - Do you have any preferences in terms of a healthcare provider or healthcare chosen not to access healthcare? Could you explain why you made those choices?
   - Are you satisfied with the healthcare services you have received at the polyclinics and general hospitals? If you use a private clinic or private hospital, are you satisfied with the services provided?
   - Are you satisfied with the current hospital and medical schemes you are eligible for?

5. **Decision-making/having a say**
   - In your family or household, how are decisions regarding your healthcare needs or visits made? Who makes these decisions?
   - Do you feel that you have a say in decision-making on the healthcare/ treatment you receive?

6. **Rights/freedom from discrimination**
   - What do you understand by the phrase 'right to health security'?
   - In your opinion, do you think you have the right to a system of health protection which provides equal opportunity to all to enjoy the highest attainable level of health?
   - Do you think you have access to essential medicines in the healthcare system in our country? Or have you faced or felt discrimination in this regard?
   - Do you think you have easy access to free health education and information?
   - Have you felt in any way discriminated by the healthcare system because of your age?
   - Have you felt in any way discriminated by the healthcare system because of your gender?

Table 1.5 Topics raised in the quantitative surveys distributed in Singapore and Malaysia

1. Demographic profile
2. Socioeconomic background, living arrangements and health status (including self-reported state of health; if diagnosed with major illnesses, and if so, what illnesses; this section also included a geriatric depression scale to self-assess the participant's sense of well-being. This section also attempted to identify the kind of social and financial support the participants receive)
3. Healthcare utilisation and care received (this included questions on the reasons for seeking healthcare, preference for the types of healthcare providers, and level of satisfaction on the healthcare provider chosen)
4. Experience in accessing outpatient care (the questions asked in this section were to gauge the accessibility, affordability and acceptability of healthcare services received)
5. Experiences in accessing inpatient care (the same questions as in outpatient care related to OPs' experience of hospitalisation).
6. Health insurance and general awareness of current healthcare schemes available (this section seeks to assess whether participants are aware of the healthcare schemes targeted at OPs and which of the schemes they are eligible for).
7. Awareness of rights (entitlement) as senior citizens (this includes questions such as if they are aware of priority to use medical services in public hospitals and clinics, and financial assistance schemes for OPs).

topical areas (Table 1.5) in an attempt to explore OPs' experiences in accessing healthcare. In Thailand and Vietnam, the analysis relied on existing national surveys of OPs' access to healthcare services, as well as the adequacy of healthcare provision in the respective countries. In Myanmar, the data was generated from the distribution of a survey questionnaire produced by HAI.

In the collection of secondary data, the researchers identified the literature on healthcare provision for OPs in the five respective countries. Aside from country-based assessments of OPs and their experiences in accessing healthcare services and their evaluation of healthcare policies in their respective countries within the human rights paradigm, legislation and relevant government departmental policy papers as well as information available on government websites were also examined with the view of assessing the extent to which a human rights-based framework is in place, particularly in terms of accessibility, quality and financial provision for health protection.

References

Albrecht, Gary L., Fitzpatrick, Ray and Susan C. Scrimshaw (eds.) (2007) *The Handbook of Social Studies in Health & Medicine*. London: Sage.

Baer, Britta, Bhushan, Anjana, Taleb, Hala Abou, Vasquez, Javier and Rebekah Thomas (2016) "The Right to Health of Older People". *Gerontologist*, 56(S2): S206–S217.

Bähler, Caroline, Huber, Carola A., Brüngger, Beat and Oliver Reich (2015) "Multi-morbidity, Health Care Utilization and Costs in an Elderly Community-Dwelling

Population: A Claims Data Based Observational Study". *BMC Health Services Research*, 15(23): 1–12.

Brownlie, Ian and Guy S. Goodwin-Gill (eds.) (2010) *Brownlie's Documents on Human Rights*. 6th Edition. Oxford: Oxford University Press.

Bunker, John (2001) "The Role of Medical Care in Contributing to Health Improvements Within Societies". *International Journal of Epidemiology*, 30(6): 1260–3.

Callahan, Daniel (1987) *Setting Limits: Medical Goals in an Aging Society*. New York: Simon and Schuster.

Chan, Moon Fai and Beverly Joan Taylor (2012) "Impact of Demographic Change, Socioeconomics, and Health Care Resources on Life Expectancy in Cambodia, Laos, and Myanmar". *Public Health Nursing*, 30(3): 183–92.

Clapham, Andrew (2006) *Human Rights Obligations of Non-State Actors*. Oxford: Oxford University Press.

Cutler, David M., Rosen, Allison B. and Sandeep Vijan (2006) "The Value of Medical Spending in the United States, 1960–2000". *New England Journal of Medicine*, 355: 920–7.

Department of Economic and Social Affairs, Population Division (2015) "World Population Ageing 2015". New York: United Nations, ST/ESA/SER.A/390. URL: <http://www.un.org/en/development/desa/population/publications/pdf/ageing/WPA2015_Report.pdf > (accessed 10 January 2018).

Department of Statistics (2016) *Population Trends 2016*. Singapore: Department of Statistics, Ministry of Trade & Industry.

Devasahayam, Theresa W. (2014) *Gender and Ageing: Southeast Asian Perspectives*. Singapore: Institute of Southeast Asian Perspectives.

Donnelly, Jack (2003) *Universal Human Rights in Theory and Practice*. Ithaca: Cornell University Press.

Donnelly, Jack and Daniel J. Whelan (2017) *International Human Rights: Dilemmas in World Politics*. Fifth Edition. New York: Westview Press.

Doron, Israel and Itai Apter (2010) "The Debate around the Need for an International Convention on the Rights of Older Persons". *The Gerontologist*, 50(5): 586–93.

Doubova, Svetlana V., Pérez-Cuevas, Ricardo, Canning, David and Michael R. Reich (2015) "Access to Healthcare and Financial Risk Protection for Older Adults in Mexico: Secondary Data Analysis of a National Survey". *BMJOpen*, 5(7): e007877.

Economic and Social Commission for Asia and the Pacific (2016) "ESCAP Population Data Sheet. Population and Development Indicators for Asia and the Pacific". URL: <www.unescap.org/resources/2016-escap-population-data-sheet> (accessed 2 February 2017).

——— (2017) "Ageing". URL: <www.unescap.org/our-work/social-development/ageing> (accessed 9 January 2018).

Estes, Carroll L. and Karen W. Linkins (2007) "Critical Perspectives on Health and Aging". In *The Handbook of Social Studies in Health & Medicine*, edited by Gary L. Albrecht, Ray Fitzpatrick and Susan C. Scrimshaw. London: Sage.

Farmer, Paul (1999) "Pathologies of Power: Rethinking Health and Human Rights". *American Journal of Public Health*, 89(10): 1486–96.

——— (2003) *Pathologies of Power: Health, Human Rights and the New War on the Poor*. Berkeley and California: University of California Press.

Fredvang, Marthe and Simon Biggs (2012) "The Rights of Older Persons: Protection and Gaps Under Human Rights Law". Paper published by Brotherhood of St Laurence and Centre for Public Policy University of Melbourne, Victoria.

Freeman, Michael (2011) *Human Rights.* Cambridge: Polity Press.

Fuchs, Victor R. (2011) *Who Shall Live?: Health, Economics and Social Choice.* Singapore: World Scientific.

Garrett, Nancy and E. Mary Martini (2007) "The Boomers Are Coming: A Total Cost of Care Model of the Impact of Population Aging on the Cost of Chronic Conditions in the United States". *Disease Management,* 10(2): 51–60.

Gerst-Emerson, Kerstin, Wong, Rebeca, Michaels-Obregon, Alejandra and Alberto Palloni (2015) "Cross-National Differences in Disability among Elders: Transitions in Disability in Mexico and the United States". *The Journals of Gerontology, Series B: Psychological Sciences &Social Sciences,* 70(5): 759–68.

Getzen, Thomas E. (1992) "Population Aging and the Growth of Healthcare Expenditures". *Journal of Gerontology,* 47(3): S98–104.

Gist, Yvonne J. and Victoria A. Velkoff (1997) "Gender and Aging: Demographic Dimensions". International Brief No. 97–3. U.S. Department of Commerce, Economics and Statistics Administration, Bureau of the Census.

Hafner-Burton, Emilie M. and Kiyoteru Tsutsui (2005) "Human Rights in a Globalizing World: The Paradox of Empty Promises". *American Journal of Sociology,* 110(5): 1373–411.

Harper, Sarah (2013) *Ageing Societies: Myths, Challenges and Opportunities.* Abingdon, Oxon: Routledge.

Henkens, Kène (2005) "Stereotyping Older Workers and Retirement: The Managers' Point of View". *Canadian Journal on Aging/La Revue canadienne du viellissement,* 24(4): 353–66.

Jones, Gavin (2013) "The Population of Southeast Asia". Asia Research Institute, Working Paper Series, No. 196. National University of Singapore.

Kasper, Judith D. (2007) "Health-Care Utilization and Barriers to Health Care". In *The Handbook of Social Studies in Health & Medicine,* edited by Gary L. Albrecht, Ray Fitzpatrick and Susan C. Scrimshaw. London: Sage.

Kespichayawattana, Jiraporn and Sutthichai Jitapunkul (2009) "Health and Health Care System for Older Persons". *Ageing International,* 33(1–4): 28–49.

Kumar, Krishna R. (2011) "Technology and Healthcare Costs". *Annals of Pediatric Cardiology,* 4(1): 84–6.

LaVeist, Thomas A. (1994) "Beyond Dummy Variables and Sample Selection: What Health Services Researchers Ought to Know About Race as a Variable". *Health Services Research,* 29(1): 1–16.

Lehnert, Thomas, Heider, Dirk, Leicht, Hanna, Heinrich, Sven, Corrieri, Sandro, Luppa, Melanie, Riedel-Heller, Steffi and Hans-Helmut König (2011) "Review: Health Care Utilization and Costs of Elderly Persons with Multiple Chronic Conditions". *Medical Care Research and Review,* 68(4): 387–420.

London, Leslie (2008) "What Is a Human-Rights Based Approach to Health and Does It Matter?". *Health and Human Rights,* 10(1): 65–80.

Mackenbach, Johan P. (1996) "The Contribution of Medical Care to Mortality Decline: McKeown Revisited". *Journal of Clinical Epidemiology,* 49: 1207–13.

Mann, Jonathan M. (2006) "Health and Human Rights If Not Now, When?". *American Journal of Public Health,* 96(11): 1940–3.

Ministry of Health (2016) "Life Expectancy in Singapore". 13 April. URL: <www.moh. gov.sg/content/moh_web/home/pressRoom/highlights/2016/life-expectancy-in-singapore0.html> (accessed 13 July 2017).

Morrissey, Mary B., Herr, Keela and Carol Levine (2015) "Public Health Imperative of the 21st Century: Innovations in Palliative Care Systems, Services, and Supports to Improve Health and Well-Being of Older Americans". *The Gerontologist*, 55(2): 245–51.

Mujahid, Ghazy (2006) "Population Ageing in East and Southeast Asia: Current Situation and Emerging Challenges". Papers in Population Ageing No. 1, UNFPA Country Technical Services Team, Bangkok, Thailand.

National Research Council (2012) "Aging and the Macroeconomy. Long-Term Implications of an Older Population". Committee on the Long-Run Macroeconomic Effects of the Aging U.S. Population. Board on Mathematical Sciences and their Applications, Division on Engineering and Physical Sciences, and Committee on Population, Division of Behavioral and Social Sciences and Education. Washington, DC: The National Academies Press.

Penchansky, Roy and J. William Thomas (1981) "The Concept of Access: Definition and Relationship to Consumer Satisfaction". *Medical Care*, 19(2): 127–40.

Posthuma, Richard A. and Michael A. Campion (2009) "Age Stereotypes in the Workplace: Common Stereotypes, Moderators, and Future Research Directions". *Journal of Management*, 35(1): 158–88.

Risse, Thomas and Kathryn Sikkink (1999) "The Socialization of International Human Rights Norms into Domestic Practices: An Introduction". In *The Power of Human Rights: International Norms and Domestic Change*, edited by Thomas Risse, Stephen C. Ropp and Kathryn Sikkink. Cambridge: Cambridge University Press.

Ryan, Susan (2014) "UN Convention for the Rights of Older Persons". Australian Human Rights Commission, 20 August. URL: <www.humanrights.gov.au/news/speeches/un-convention-rights-older-persons> (accessed 23 July 2017).

Schulman, Kevin A., Rubenstein, L. Elizabeth, Chesley, Francis D. and John M. Eisenberg (1995) "The Roles of Race and Socioeconomic Factors in Health Services Research". *Health Services Research*, 30 (1 Pt 2): 179–95.

Shahid, Ahmed and Hilary Yerbury (2014) "A Case Study of the Socialization of Human Rights Language and Norms in Maldives: Process, Impact and Challenges". *Journal of Human Rights Practice*, 6(2): 281–305.

Simmons, Beth A. (2009) *Mobilizing for Human Rights: International Law in Domestic Politics*. New York: Cambridge University Press.

United Nations Population Fund and HelpAge International (2012) *Ageing in the Twenty-First Century – A Celebration and a Challenge*. London: UNFPA and HelpAge International.

World Bank (2017) *World Development Indicators 2016*. Washington, DC: World Bank.

World Health Organization (2017) "Human Rights and Health". URL: <www.who.int/mediacentre/factsheets/fs323/en/> (accessed 10 January 2018).

——— (2018a) "10 Facts on Health Inequities and their Causes". 27 April. URL: <www.who.int/features/factfiles/health_inequities/en/> (accessed 10 January 2018).

——— (2018b) "SDG 3: Ensure Healthy Lives and Promote Wellbeing for All at All Ages". URL: <www.who.int/sdg/targets/en/> (accessed 10 January 2018).

2 Singapore

Theresa W. Devasahayam

2.1 Introduction

Singapore has undergone rapid economic growth in the last few decades, earning itself the reputation of being an 'economic miracle' in Asia. For over five decades starting in 1960, the country's per capita gross domestic product grew more than 100-fold (Bloomberg 2015) and for several decades, the country has enjoyed the highest rate of economic growth in comparison to its ASEAN neighbours. In tandem with Singapore's economic growth in the first few decades since its independence in 1965 have been shifts in its demographic profile. In particular, the proportion of its elderly has steadily grown while fertility rates have seen a significant decline (Jones 1995). These demographic shifts in part could be attributed to improvements in medical technologies and higher standards of living leading to lower mortality rates. Moreover, social changes such as increasing levels of education among women and increasing labour force participation rates have led to falling fertility rates, thereby affecting the age distribution of the population (Jones 2009). Furthermore, it has been asserted that the country's anti-natalist policy in the 1970s has been responsible for the declining fertility rates in the last few decades and that measures to reverse such policies have had little success in turning the situation around because they have been implemented too late (Jones 2009; Jones, Straughan and Chan 2009).

Apart from falling fertility rates, an analysis of the longitudinal population trends in Singapore point to a steady increase in life expectancy. Since the country's independence in 1965, life expectancy has been inching up. In 1970, life expectancy at birth for the Singaporean female was 67.8 years while for the Singaporean male, it was 64.1 years (Department of Statistics 2017a). There was an increase in life expectancy for both sexes in the following decades; in 1990, life expectancy soared to 77.6 years and 73.1 years for females and males, respectively, and in 2012, life expectancy for the Singaporean female was 84.3 years while for the male it was 79.8 years; in 2016, life expectancy went up further to 85.1 years for females and 80.6 years for males. According to the United Nations Population Prospects 2015 (United Nations, Department of Economic and Social Affairs, Population Division 2015), Singapore is ranked fifth in the world for highest life expectancy at 82.6 years, with Hong Kong ranked first (83.7 years), Japan second (83.3 years), Italy in third place (82.8 years), followed by Switzerland coming in fourth place (82.7 years). In fact, overall life expectancy reached 83 years in 2016 from 80 years in 2006 (Department of Statistics 2017b).

The proportion of the elderly, defined as persons aged 65 years and older, has only been growing steadily since 1965. In that year, it was recorded that 2.5 percent of the country's population fell into the elderly cohort. Since then, the proportion of elderly has swelled to 6 percent in 1990, 7.2 percent in 2000 and 8.8 percent in 2009 (Department of Statistics 2014; Department of Statistics 2009, as cited in the Report on the State of the Elderly in Singapore 2008/2009). In fact, it was by 2000 that Singapore had become an ageing society, according to the World Health Organization definition of ageing, and in 2014, the proportion of this age group had reached 11.2 percent (Department of Statistics 2014) and by 2017, 13 percent, respectively (Department of Statistics 2017b). According to population projections, by 2030, the elderly will have reached 22.6 percent of the country's total population (Ministry of Social and Family Development 2014), while by 2050, this figure will jump to 32 percent (World Bank estimate, as cited in Reisman 2009). In another report, it has been said that in less than 10 years, Singapore could join more than 30 countries in the world to become a "super-aged" nation, where 20 percent of the population is 65 years and above (Kotwani 2017). In fact, data from the Department of Statistics published in 2014 demonstrated that the proportion of the very old (age 75 and above) has grown from 1.3 percent in 1980 to 4.2 percent in 2014, and that Singapore will become a super-aged society in 2026 (Tan 2015). On this, it must be said that not only has the proportion of the elderly population grown but the elderly population has also grown older.

Of concern to the Singapore government is the pressures a fast ageing population will have on the public resources of the country. Salient in the ageing policy of Singapore is that it has consistently adopted a policy of "ageing in place" with various initiatives established to fulfil this policy and, in turn, adopting a whole-of-Government and whole-of-society approach to building a Nation for All Ages. In this regard, Singapore's policy on ageing has identified the family as the primary site for eldercare. In this case, the family acts as the primary support system for ageing individuals, and concomitantly housing and health policies reinforce this idea. For example, Singapore's housing policy incentivises individuals to live in close proximity (although not necessarily in the same residential unit) to their parents through the allocation of grants to home buyers. In addition, individuals with elderly parents are granted income tax reliefs, with a higher amount granted to those who are co-residing with their parents than those who are not living together. It is this network of support structures which places the family at the centre of the support framework for eldercare, and in cases when the family is unable to do its part and execute its role in providing care towards the older person (OP), the community and government to varying degrees would step in with the community first providing assistance, failing which the government becomes the last resort (Goh 2006). It is this support structure framework for eldercare which has come to be known as the "many helping hands" approach (Mehta 2002). By the same token, the government maintains that an elderly person should depend on his/her family in times of a health crisis and health policies are designed in such a way that an elderly person's financial expenses can be borne by family members, a point that will be picked up later in the chapter.

2.2   Health status of Singaporean older persons

Health screening practices were found to be more prevalent among adults in the 60–69 age group as they are more likely to have had their blood checked for chronic diseases compared to those among the younger age groups. In Singapore, chronic diseases are a major source of morbidity and mortality among OPs. Diabetes mellitus, hypertension, hyperlipidemia (lipid disorders) and stroke were identified as the major chronic diseases under the Chronic Disease Management Programme (CDMP) first set up in 2006. In 2008, asthma and chronic obstructive pulmonary disease (COPD) were added to the list, and in 2009, schizophrenia and major depression and in 2011, bipolar disorder and dementia, respectively. In January 2014, osteoarthritis, benign prostatic hyperplasia, anxiety, Parkinson's disease and nephrosis/nephritis were also listed as chronic diseases under the programme and in 2015, epilepsy, osteoporosis, psoriasis and rheumatoid arthritis. As of the time of writing (2017), there were a total of 19 chronic diseases under CDMP (Ministry of Health 2015a).

In 2015, it was said that one in four Singaporeans aged above 65 years old developed a chronic disease (Boh 2016). The Singapore Burden of Disease Study published in 2010 reported that individuals aged 65 and above suffered from 35.5 percent of the entire burden of disease and injury inflicting Singaporeans (Ministry of Health 2014a). Among this group, cardiovascular diseases, mostly ischaemic heart disease and stroke, accounted for 30 percent, followed by cancer at 22 percent and neurological and sense disorders, mostly Alzheimer's and other dementias, vision disorders and loss of hearing at 15 percent. The other diseases hitting OPs include: chronic respiratory diseases (7 percent), respiratory infections (6 percent), diabetes mellitus (5 percent), genito-urinary diseases (5 percent), digestive diseases (2 percent) and others (8 percent) (Ministry of Health 2014a).

Among both older men and women, the same study revealed that ischaemic heart disease and stroke were the top two leading specific causes of burden. Among older men, however, lung cancer, chronic obstructive pulmonary disease and Alzheimer's and other dementias constituted the third, fourth and fifth burden of disease while among older women, they were Alzheimer's and other dementias, lower respiratory tract infections, and diabetes mellitus, in that order (Ministry of Health 2014a). Overall the report also indicated that the percentage of the burden of disease among elderly women was slightly higher than among elderly men (5.5 percent). While the difference in the burden of cardiovascular disease was equal between the sexes, elderly men were found to experience a greater share of chronic respiratory diseases and cancer. Compared with older men, however, Wu and Chan (2011) found that the current genera-tion of older women aged 65 and above is more likely to experience declines in health status and well-being as they get older because of a higher risk of chronic illnesses such as heart disease, diabetes, stroke and high blood pressure, resulting from longer life expectancy and a lower likelihood of access to appro-priate health and social care.

In terms of self-reported health, the National Survey of Senior Citizens of 2011 (Kang, Tan and Yap 2013) showed distinct differences between older men and women. Among 5000 respondents participating in the study con-ducted by the Institute of Policy Studies and commissioned by the Elderly and Disability Group, Ministry of Social and Family Development, it was found that 76.4 percent of those aged 55 and above rated their health as "good" or "very good", whereas only 2.7 percent rated their health as "poor" and the remaining of 20.9 percent indicated that their health was "fair". The same survey also found that those aged 75 and older were more likely to rate their health as "poor" (5.2 percent) compared to those in the younger age cohorts. In the same survey, males aged 65 and above were more likely to rate their health positively among those indicating "very good" compared with females – a pattern found in the younger age cohort of 55–64 years as well (Table 2.1). This pattern reinforced the finding in the Global Burden of Disease Study 2015 that Singaporean men have the highest life expectancy among males in the world (GBD 2015 DALYs and HALE Collaborators 2016), although women reported to have had generally better health behaviour (Chua 2009).

The survey also found that nearly four out of ten (45 percent) in the age group 55 to 64 years claimed not to have any medical condition, while 29.5 per-cent of those in the age group 65 to 74 years and 19.4 percent of those aged 75 and older indicated likewise (Kang et al. 2013). Data from the survey also showed that the most common medical condition was high blood pressure

Table 2.1 Self-rated health status, 2011 (percent)

Self-rated health status	Total (55+)		55–64			65–74			75 and above		
	M	F	Total	M	F	Total	M	F	Total	M	F
Poor	2.3	3.1	2.1	2.2	1.9	2.5	1.2	3.6	5.2	4.3	5.8
Fair	21.2	20.6	16.8	19.3	14.4	23.8	23.0	24.4	30.4	26.2	33.3
Good	63.4	67.2	67.1	63.1	71.1	66.0	65.9	66.1	58.5	59.9	57.6
Very good	13.2	9.1	14.0	15.3	12.7	7.7	9.9	6.0	5.8	9.6	3.3
Total	100.0	100.0	100.0	100.0	100.0	100.0	100.0	100.0	100.0	100.0	100.0

Source: Kang et al. (2013)

(47 percent), followed by high cholesterol (39 percent), diabetes (16 percent), arthritis (11 percent) and eye/vision problem (5 percent).

Because mobility is a critical issue as age catches up on an individual, relevant questions on this issue were often incorporated into surveys. According to the National Survey of Senior Citizens 2011, nearly 96 percent of the respondents were ambulant and physically independent, while the proportion increased to 98 percent if we were to include those who regularly resorted to using walking aids (Kang et al. 2013). Of the remaining 2 percent, 1.4 percent either required some assistance whereas 0.4 percent required full physical assistance and 0.2 percent were bed-ridden.

In another survey, the General Household Survey 2015 (Department of Statistics 2016), it was found that 87 percent of the resident elderly population in Singapore were ambulant, while 10.5 percent were semi-ambulant and 2.4 percent were non-ambulant. Consistently, there were more women than men who were either semi-ambulant or non-ambulant. The data is consistent with worldwide trends as while women tend to live longer than men, they tend to live longer years in disability compared with men. In other words, morbidity rates are higher among women compared with men. These differentials are critical for two reasons: first, it reflects on an individual's ability to contribute to the household income and provide support to family members; second, these differentials demonstrate older men's and women's need for support.

2.3   Healthcare system and policies focusing on older persons

In Singapore, the Ministry of Health has been tasked with ensuring quality and affordable basic medical services for all by regulating both the public and private providers of healthcare (Ministry of Health 2013). Government initiatives to address the needs of an ageing population started as early as 1982. Several high-level committees were formed to study the country's ageing trends and it was then that there was a recognition that the country's demographic trends were changing. In 1982–1984, a "Committee on the Problems of the Aged" was convened, chaired by the then Health Minister, Howe Yoon Chong, to examine the implications of an ageing population and the solutions to be adopted to tackle the accompanying challenges (Goh 2006). The following years saw the establishment of similar committees: The Advisory Council on the Aged (1988–1989), the National Advisory Council on the Family and the Aged (NACFA) (1989–1998), the Inter-Ministerial Committee on the Ageing Population (IMC) (initially set up in 1998 and reconstituted in 2003), the Committee on Ageing Issues (CAI) (2004–2006) and the Tripartite Committee on Employability of Older Workers (2005). It was in 1997 that an Inter-Ministerial Committee on Health Care for the Elderly (IMCHCE) was set up to examine the potential demands an ageing population placed on the healthcare system in Singapore and the affordability of a healthcare system to OPs.

In 1999, the Ministerial Committee on Ageing (MCA) – a high-level committee comprising government ministers – oversaw the implementation of policies and programmes on ageing to execute the vision of Successful Ageing (Zhang, Heng and Chye 2017) through (a) improving the employment and financial security of OPs; (b) enabling "ageing-in-place"; (c) providing holistic and affordable healthcare and eldercare; and (d) promoting active ageing. In 2007, the Committee on Ageing Issues recommended establishing the Council for Third Age (C3A) which oversees public education and outreach on active ageing. The Council is also responsible for the administering of the Golden Opportunities! (GO!) Fund which provides seed money for projects to encourage active ageing such as creating opportunities for volunteerism among the elderly and providing opportunities for them to broaden their social networks. In addition, the government maintains the position that the elderly should continue to be active participants in the labour force. Under the re-employment legislation called the Retirement and Re-employment Act (RRA) which came into effect in January 2012, employers are obliged to offer their retiring workers re-employment until age 65 (Ministry of Manpower 2017a). However from 1 July 2017, employers by law must offer re-employment up to the age of 67 to eligible employees who turn 62 (Ministry of Manpower 2017b).

By and large, policies in Singapore, whether or not they are targeted at the elderly, tend to emphasise self-reliance, self-sufficiency and individual responsibility although there is universal coverage and no one person is denied access to receiving healthcare. This anti-welfare stance extends to the elderly; individuals are expected to take care of oneself in old age through the Central Provident Fund (CPF) system (Lee 2014). In keeping with the policy that the family is the primary site of eldercare, adult children are allowed to use their Medisave savings from their CPF towards the healthcare expenses of their elderly parents so as to better care for their parents in old age. In 2012, Ministry of Health statistics showed that about 4,600 CPF members aged 60 years old and above withdrew an average of $2,000 from their own Medisave accounts to cover their parents' medical bills (Ministry of Health 2013). However, given the rising costs of healthcare and that many people do not have adequate savings for retirement because the bulk would have been channelled into purchasing their homes (Koh, Mitchell, Tanuwidjaja and Fong 2008), additional health schemes have been installed to help OPs access healthcare. Thus, in Singapore, the twin factors of health and social security policies determine healthcare access.

2.3.1 Health schemes for the elderly

The healthcare system in Singapore is predicated on the "twin philosophies of individual responsibility and affordable healthcare for all" (Ministry of Health 2017a). Essentially, the system is characterised by different levels of protection on the basic premise that no one individual is denied access to basic healthcare services because of the lack of funds. A caveat must be made that underlying the system is the assumption of individual responsibility for one's healthcare needs at every level in keeping with the state's anti-welfare position.

2.3.2 Subsidies

The Singapore healthcare system is marked by three tiers of protection. The first tier of protection is provided by government subsidies of up to 80 percent of the total bill in acute public hospital wards (Ministry of Health 2017a). This is achieved through universal access with co-payment to ensure appropriate care (Ministry of Health 2017a).

2.3.3 Medisave

The second tier of protection is provided through what is called Medisave, essentially comprising a compulsory individual national savings scheme enabling all Singaporeans to cover their share of medical treatment for smaller medical bills (Ministry of Health 2017a). In Singapore, working individuals and their employers contribute a portion of the monthly wages into this savings account which accumulates over the years and is saved for future medical needs. The scheme, which is part of the broader comprehensive social security savings plan called the CPF to which all employed individuals contribute, is portable across jobs and after retirement.

As of 1 January 2016, the Medisave Minimum Sum (MMS) was removed and replaced with the Basic Healthcare Sum (BHS). Among CPF members who withdraw their monies from the Ordinary and Special Accounts (OSA) upon reaching age 55, they will no longer be required to top up their Medisave Account to ensure a Minimum Sum. For the Basic Healthcare Sum (BHS), the minimum has been set at $52,000 from 1 January 2017 for all CPF members (Ministry of Manpower 2017b). As of 2016, the average Medisave balance per account was Singapore $24,200 (Ministry of Health 2017b).

Among those with insufficient Medisave funds, the option is to rely on immediate kin by tapping into the latter's Medisave account. Women are more likely to tap on the Medisave accounts of their kin since they would have had fewer savings in their own CPF accounts or may not even have had CPF accounts in the first place because of not having worked or as a result of having left the workforce to provide care for their children or elderly parents. Because the scheme restricts how the funds may be utilised, individuals may end up using personal funds to pay for their medical bills and in dire cases wipe out their own savings should they come from the lower-income group. For example, Medisave funds can be used if the patient stays in the hospital for at least 8 hours (unless the patient is admitted for day surgery) (Ministry of Health 2016).

2.3.4 Medishield

The third level of protection is provided by MediShield, which has now been renamed Medishield Life (Ministry of Health 2017a). This low-cost catastrophic medical insurance scheme enables Singaporeans to risk-pool the financial risks of major illnesses. Because this scheme demands deductibles and co-payment, individual responsibility for one's health is emphasised. From 1 November 2015, it became mandatory for all citizens and Singapore Permanent Residents to become Medishield policyholders (Ministry of Health 2015b). In 2014, there were 3.6 million Medishield policyholders (Ministry of Health 2017c). In that same year, a total of 2,485,000 Medishield policyholders had supplemented their basic healthcare coverage with integrated private insurance policies ("Integrated Shield Plans") (Ministry of Health 2017c). But before any policyholder purchases the add-on private Integrated Shield Plan, they must be a policyholder of the basic Medishield plan.

2.3.5 ElderShield

Non-mandatory contributory health schemes have also been installed for the protection of OPs. One such scheme is the ElderShield, a severe disability insurance scheme which provides basic financial protection to those who need long-term care, primarily targeted at OPs. Offered to all 40-year-old Singaporeans, an OP under this scheme receives a monthly cash payout to help pay the out-of-pocket expenses for the care of a severely-disabled person. In this case, severe disability is defined as clinically assessed failure in three or more activities of daily living (ADL).

Currently, there are two ElderShield schemes: ElderShield300 and ElderShield400, and premiums are purchased through private insurers. Singapore Citizens and Permanent Residents who join ElderShield after September 2007 will only be eligible to apply for the ElderShield400 scheme. The payouts for both schemes are Singapore $300 for a maximum of 60 months under ElderShield300, and Singapore $400 for a maximum of 72 months under ElderShield400 (Central Provident Fund 2017). In 2016, there were a total of 1,279,000 policyholders (Ministry of Health 2017b). "ElderShield Supplements" allows policyholders to enhance the disability benefits coverage offered by the basic ElderShield product. 2016 saw 437,000 policyholders for this ElderShield product (Ministry of Health 2017b).

Among those who do not have sufficient savings, this scheme will be made available to them only should they have immediate kin who are able to undertake the payment of the policy on their behalf. Moreover, the payout term is capped at five years for ElderShield300 and six years for ElderShield 400; in other words, the insured will only be covered for a limited period (Central Provident Fund 2017). Another disadvantage is that ElderShield only covers catastrophic illnesses or accidents. Should an elderly person require assistance for preventive diagnosis, care or treatment, such a scheme may not benefit him/her. Hence while ElderShield may be considered as an additional scheme to help the elderly, its protection as a safety net is limited. Women are also disadvantaged under this scheme; the premiums they pay are higher than men because they are more likely to suffer from higher levels of morbidity compared with men (Income 2017).

2.3.6 Medifund

For the poorer Singapore residents, Medifund, a medical endowment fund, was set up to ensure that those who cannot afford to pay their medical bills through Medisave and MediShield will be covered. In 2016, there were 1,136,000 applications for Medifund. In 2015, there were 1,097,000 applicants up from 1,006,000 in 2014 (Ministry of Health 2017b), 587,000 in 2012, and 518,000 in 2011 (Ministry of Health 2014a), indicating growing numbers among the elderly who are struggling with covering their healthcare expenses. For the elderly poor, in particular, a quarterly cash supplement to the bottom 20 percent of Singaporeans aged 65 and above was implemented. Moreover, these are individuals who have had low incomes throughout their lives and who currently have little or no family support.

2.3.7 *Pioneer generation package*

The scheme provides healthcare benefits to "pioneers" for life. Created in 2014, the Pioneer Generation Package (PGP) was created with the intention of recognising the pioneer generation for their contribution and dedication to building Singapore. Under the scheme, all pioneers will receive special subsidies at CHAS (Community Health Assist Scheme) General Practitioners (GPs) and dental clinics. Pioneers will also be entitled to receive an additional 50 percent off at polyclinics and Specialist Outpatient Clinics and an additional 50 percent off subsidised medications at polyclinics and Specialist Outpatient Clinics (as of January 2015). On top of those subsidies, pioneers with moderate or severe disabilities can receive a cash payment of $1,200 per year to help with their care expenses (Ministry of Health 2017d). In addition, pioneers receive Medisave top-ups of Singapore $200–800 annually for life (as of July 2014) and special premium subsidies for the Pioneers' MediShield Life Premiums (as of late 2015). For those aged 80 and above in 2014, premiums will be fully covered while those aged 65 to 79 need only pay 50 percent of their premiums under MediShield. It was estimated that 450,000 Singaporeans benefited from this scheme (Government of Singapore 2018; Neo 2014).

2.3.8 *Silver support scheme and Community Health Assist Scheme (CHAS)*

In 2015, more assistance was rendered to the poor and needy elderly in the form of the Silver Support Scheme—a long-term scheme to help this group of elderly to cope with their daily expenses. This scheme is provided on top of CHAS rolled out by the Ministry of Health and aimed at specific age and income cohorts among the larger population including OPs. This scheme enables Singapore Citizens from lower- and middle-income households to receive subsidies for medical and dental care at participating GPs and dental clinics near their homes from 1 January 2014 (CHAS n.d.). All Singapore Citizens (regardless of age) eligible for this scheme have to meet the household monthly income per person of $1,800 and below.

2.3.9 *The Agency for Integrated Care (AIC)*

Aside from these healthcare policies and schemes, the healthcare system underwent a major revamp in the area of intermediate and long-term care in recent years. The Agency for Integrated Care (AIC) was formed as an independent corporate entity under MOH Holdings (MOHH) in 2009 to assume the role of National Care Integrator to coordinate and facilitate the placement of elderly sick to nursing homes and chronic sick units (Agency for Integrated Care 2016). In seeking to create a vibrant care community and enable people to live well and age gracefully, AIC works with Community Care. The Wellness Programme was also created with the aim of encouraging the elderly to stay healthy through physical activities and social engagement (The Sunday Times 17 June 2013).

2.4 Assessing health security among older persons in Singapore

2.4.1 Assessment methods

Primary data for the study was conducted from June 2016 to January 2017.

The survey questionnaire, originally designed for the purposes of distribution in Myanmar was modified for the Singapore context and distributed to a total of 120 respondents. Of the total number, only 113 survey questionnaires proved to be valid for use in the final analysis as the rest were found to have discrepancies and gaps. In most cases, it was found that although the respondent had consented to participating in the study, for those questions which were not completed, the respondent chose not to wish to divulge information.

Although in Singapore those considered elderly are 65 years and above, following the other countries in the study, OPs were defined as those 60 years and above.

The respondents for the survey questionnaire portion of the study were sourced through three voluntary welfare organisations (VWOs) working on eldercare issues as well as a local mosque. Other respondents included friends of the author who met the criteria to participate in the study as well as their kin and friends. In that case, the snowball technique was used to identify respondents.

The respondents comprised Singaporean citizens of the three major ethnic groups: Chinese (84), Malays (17) and Indians (12). In terms of the gender of the respondents, there were 72 females and 41 males altogether. Because the sample size was skewed with larger numbers of females participating in the study, it should be noted that this affects the final analysis of the data.

The respondents came from households of different income levels. For income level, housing was used as a proxy. The majority of respondents lived in Housing and Development Board (HDB) flats or government-subsidised housing ranging from three to five room flats. A much smaller number lived in one-room rental flats owned by the government while the rest lived in private condominiums and houses or landed property. The majority of respondents were retirees while only a handful engaged in waged work. Among those who worked, nearly all were men, as was found in previous studies (Chan and Yap 2009). The majority of respondents had high school education while a smaller number had primary and tertiary education. Most of the respondents in the study lived in extended households although there was a significant portion who lived alone or with an elderly spouse with children living nearby – trends that were found in other surveys as well (Ministry of Social and Family Development 2014).

Qualitative data was also collected for the study. Face-to-face interviews were conducted among 22 respondents among whom nine were Chinese, eight were Malays and five were Indians. Translators were used for the Chinese respondents. Some Malay respondents were also interviewed in their native language by a translator since they felt more comfortable using their mother tongue. Although the author understands Malay, she relied on the translator especially since the respondent was known to the translator previously.

Verbal consent was received by all respondents participating in both the quantitative and qualitative components of the study. Consent was received by the respondents at the start of the data collection process. The research assistant collecting the data also explained to each respondent that he or she could at any time withdraw from the study, if he or she wished, at the start of the interview. To protect the identity of the respondents participating in the study, the acronym, IDI has been used throughout the chapter.

Interviews for both the survey questionnaire and the face-to-face interviews were conducted either on the premises of the VWOs, void decks of HDB flats or in the homes of the respondents. On average, it took about 45 minutes to complete a survey questionnaire and at least an hour to complete the face-to-face interview.

Several research assistants helped in the distribution of the survey questionnaire. They also assisted in translation and transcribing the face-to-face interviews. A research assistant was also hired to key in the data collected into an excel file for analysis purposes. A separate research assistant was later hired to analyse the survey data and generate tables and figures.

Secondary data were also utilised in the analysis. Primary data available on the Ministry of Health website was used. The analysis for the chapter also relied on several surveys on the elderly conducted by various government departments and academic institutes in Singapore. These sources and reports on the elderly are as follows: (a) "Baby-Boomers Survey", Survey commissioned by the Ministry of Social and Family Development (MSF), Angelique Chan and Yap Mui Teng, Singapore, 2009; (b) National Survey of Senior Citizens. Singapore: Institute of Policy Studies (2013); (c) Population Trends 2014. Singapore: Department of Statistics (2014); and (d) "Ageing Families in Singapore". Insight Series Paper 02/2015, Ministry of Social and Family Development (2014).

2.4.2 *Key findings*

Accessibility

Being a city-state with a well-developed infrastructure, healthcare services are easily accessible. The healthcare delivery system in Singapore is characterised by a mixed delivery model. The system is dominated by the public sector which delivers 80 percent of the acute care in this sector whereas primary care is provided mainly by private sector providers serving 80 percent of the market (Ministry of Health 2017a). Voluntary welfare organisations are involved in providing different services in the step-down care sector (e.g. nursing homes, community hospitals and hospices). These organisations receive partial funding from the government while relying on public donations as well. Scattered across the country are several polyclinics with at least one in each district. Thus, a range of healthcare providers are available, including public hospitals and polyclinics, private hospitals and GPs, and VWO-operated clinics, and so forth.

Among the respondents, it was found that polyclinics are the healthcare facility most often accessed (44 percent) (Figure 2.1). Conversely, those surveyed were least likely to seek medical assistance from a Specialist Outpatient Centre (3 percent), private hospital (3 percent) and National Specialty Centre (2 percent).

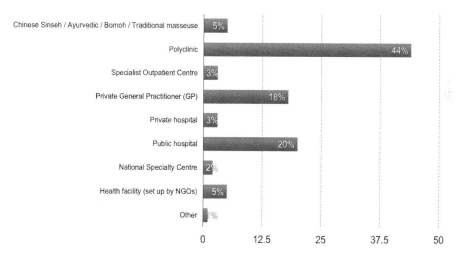

Figure 2.1 Where did you go when being injured or ill?
Source: Own calculations from the survey
Note: n = 106

In the face-to-face interviews, it appeared that proximity was a key factor in decisions made in the choice of healthcare provider one would access. A male respondent had this to say:

> I go to the GP nearby . . . the GP is so close . . . he is in the next block . . . I know him for a long time. . . . We end up talking about other things . . . I don't go to the polyclinic . . . although it is relatively accessible . . . the GP is closer. . . . Also, when I am not feeling well, I rather not drive . . . it is easier to go downstairs (that is, to the GP).
>
> (IDI, Indian Male, 67 years old)

The mode of transport used to access healthcare services also influences the decision on which healthcare provider one should seek medical assistance. Interestingly enough because this male respondent prefers not to drive to the polyclinic because he is unwell, he opts for the general practitioner or GP who lives close to him.

The duration in which one would take to access a healthcare provider was also an important factor for most of the respondents. More than one-third of the respondents (35 percent) indicated that it took them 5–10 minutes to access a healthcare provider, indicating that time spent travelling to seek medical assistance was important in the kind of healthcare provider one would use (Figure 2.2). One out of four respondents (26 percent) indicated that they travelled 15–20 minutes to reach the healthcare provider they most often used. Close to one-quarter (23 percent) was willing to travel 25–30 minutes to reach a healthcare provider.

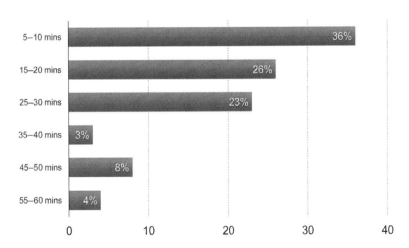

Figure 2.2 How long it took you to get there

Source: Own calculations from the survey

Note: n = 106

From the figure above, the majority of respondents (83 percent) was found to be willing to spend an average of 10–25 minutes to reach a healthcare provider. For the majority, public transportation was used, and the travel time would have also included waiting time. Far fewer used private transport such as a car.

Among those who chose to use the polyclinics most often should they fall ill because it was the closest healthcare facility were aware that there were limitations in using this healthcare provider since polyclinics were only open during office hours. Among them, they were aware that they could not "afford to fall ill at night or over the weekends". One Chinese male respondent said:

> I usually go to the polyclinic . . . it is my first choice because it is most convenient as it is close to my place . . . if you go to a private clinic, you pay so much more . . . but the downside is that you cannot access the polyclinic at night or during the weekends . . . in fact, better not fall ill over the weekends.
>
> (IDI, Chinese Male, 68 years old)

In Singapore, the only public healthcare facility operating at night or over the weekends are the Accident & Emergency (A&E) departments at the hospitals. People are, however, discouraged from turning up at the A&E facilities to seek for medical attention especially for mild ailments like a cough or cold at night and instead have patients wait until the next day to use either the services provided at the polyclinics or any other healthcare provider. In this case, a flat fee of Singapore $115 is meted out so as to discourage people from using the A&E facilities at the public hospitals.

The data also indicated that there were no obvious obstacles to accessing healthcare for the average OP. But it must be said that this only applies to outpatient care but not for chronic illnesses because of the costs involved. This point was reiterated by one interviewee:

> There is no sense of discrimination because of age . . . now they are doing a lot more for the senior citizens . . . if you compare now to before, old people now have more coverage.
>
> (IDI, Indian Male, 64 years old)

Affordability

In Singapore, healthcare expenditure on the part of the government has been steadily rising over the last few years. In 2015, the operating expenditure was $7,520 million up from $5,872 million in 2014 (Table 2.2) (Ministry of Health 2017b). The government's health expenditure also increased from 2.1 percent of the country's GDP in 2015 from 1.8 percent in 2014 (Table 2.2). If Singapore was compared to other OECD countries similar in developmental status and population size, the amount of funds channelled into healthcare is far less. According to the Ministry of Health (2017a)

Table 2.2 Government health expenditure, 2013–2015

Indicators	2013	2014	2015
Operating Expenditure ($m)	5,044	5,872	7,520
Development Expenditure ($m)	723	1,147	1,413
Government Health Expenditure[1] (as percent of GDP)	5,938	7,221.3	8,610.4
Government Health Expenditure[1] (as percent of GDP)	1.6	1.8	2.1

Source: Ministry of Health (2017b).

Note: [1] Includes expenditure from endowment funds and excludes government transfer

website, the Singapore government admits that its "national healthcare expenditure of about 4 % of our GDP . . . is low among developed countries" although it is expecting to raise this expenditure in future because of its ageing population.

In terms of government health expenditure per person, this too has been going up over the years. In 2013, the sum was $787 per person while in 2014, it was $905 and in 2015, $1,104 (Ministry of Health 2014b). In spite of the increase in government expenditure per person, the country's medical inflation rate was reported to have been 15 percent, which was much higher than the global estimate of 10 percent (Wai 2016). Given the climate of rising healthcare costs, people are encouraged to purchase health insurance plans with riders to cover various out-of-pocket expenses. Since the PGP came into effect, the elderly can rely on substantial subsidies, bringing their healthcare expenditure down to what one elderly woman said was "such a small sum" compared to what she would have had to pay before the scheme was in place.

Among the elderly who were surveyed and interviewed for this project, it was evident that the most pressing issue facing them was the cost of healthcare. For this reason, the majority of respondents sought to go to the polyclinic as first port of call, especially those who are self-paying:

> I will go to the polyclinic . . . I go through them if I want to get the subsidy . . . unless you want to go to the private doctor . . . or specialist . . . I think it is all the same. . . . It is a matter of price. . . . Normal polyclinics have good doctors . . . I usually go straight to the polyclinics . . . if I need a specialist . . . I go to the polyclinic to get a referral letter.
>
> (IDI, Chinese Female, 66 years old)

Among this group of respondents, some were more specific about the costs incurred in accessing healthcare, although they were reflecting on outpatient care.

> Yes, I think it is [affordable] . . . only because of the subsidies . . . under the Pioneer Generation Package. . . . Before if I paid $30 for the flu medication and some other illness, now it is only $8 . . . one time, I only paid

$3. . . . For a pioneer, it is worth it . . . I also went to the orthopaedic doctor once and the bill from $100 became $25.

(IDI, Chinese Male, 65 years old)

However, when asked if they thought the treatment costs was within their expectation, an overwhelming majority (85 percent) out of a total of 102 respondents said that they thought it was, while 6 percent said "no" and 8 percent said that they did not know (Figure 2.3). During the face-to-face interviews, however, it was found that the majority thought that the fees they had paid were "within their expectation" although when probed, many did not know how much exactly the services they had received actual costs since they had also received subsidies through the PGP or other schemes for which they were eligible.

On the same topic of affordability, a few interviewees during the face-to-face interviews, however, said that they thought that healthcare was unaffordable for chronic diseases, especially if they felt an OP did not have adequate health coverage. One man made this comment:

It [healthcare] is not [affordable], especially for chronic cases . . . it is no problem for me because I have a CSC (Civil Service Card) card . . . I don't have to think twice . . . but I know people who struggle . . . a lot of them struggle . . . one time, I attended a case . . . the boy was 13 years old . . . he had an asthma attacked and the boy died . . . I scolded the mother . . . I was a policeman then . . . I realised after that that they were very poor and they could not bring the boy to the hospital on time . . . I was at the home for some time. . . . It was a one-room rental flat and the house was spartan. . . .

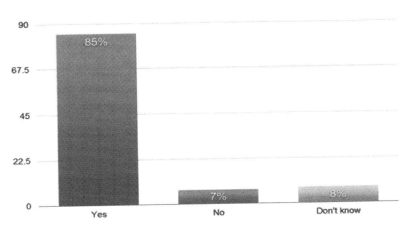

Figure 2.3 Cost of treatment within expectation

Source: Own calculations from the survey

Note: n = 102

I was talking to the mother . . . and she was crying . . . I felt bad later on for scolding the mother.

(IDI, Chinese Male, 68 years old)

In relation to hospitalisation costs, a much smaller proportion of OPs (70 percent) felt that the hospitalisation cost was within their expectation, suggesting that they might have thought that the bills had far exceeded what they had expected and that they thought of the costs involved to be far more expensive than they had thought (Figure 2.4).

Many also spoke of dental care not being affordable while admitting that this was also critical to overall health.

Healthcare is unaffordable for the majority in this country . . . as they say, better to die than to get sick in this country . . . as an extension, dental care is very expensive . . . to fill a tooth costs X number of dollars . . . in Malaysia, it is one-third the amount you pay in Singapore . . . if you have a big hole or you need four fillings, it will be very expensive.

(IDI, Chinese Male, 62 years old)

The study also discovered that without the help of family members, the majority of OPs surveyed would not have been able to afford healthcare in spite of the different schemes that have been set up to enable the elderly to access subsidies. Among a total of 113 respondents, close to half (49 percent) were dependent on others to undertake their healthcare expenses, whereas only about one in three (29 percent) were able to pay for their healthcare bills on their

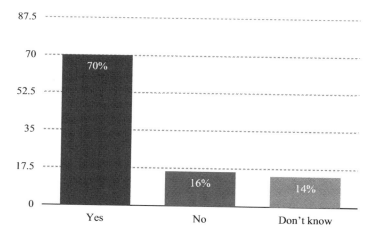

Figure 2.4 Cost of hospitalisation within expectation
Source: Own calculations from the survey
Note: n = 43

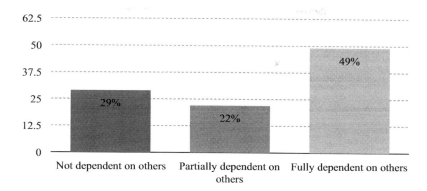

Figure 2.5 Economic dependency

Source: Own calculations from the survey

Note: n = 113

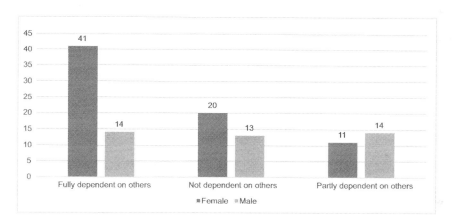

Figure 2.6 Economic dependence by gender

Source: Own calculations from the survey

Note: n (male) = 41; n (female) = 72

own (Figure 2.5) while the remainder were partially dependent on others. This trend is to be expected since the majority of OPs are not working for a variety of reasons and might have inadequate savings.

Examining the data by gender, it was found that women were consistently economically dependent on others compared with men although it must be cautioned that the study surveyed more women than men. Having said that among the total sample of 113 respondents, women were overwhelmingly dependent on others financially compared to men (Figure 2.6).

In spite of OPs struggling with finances, the study found that 35 percent of those surveyed had paid for the bulk of their medicines themselves (Figure 2.7)

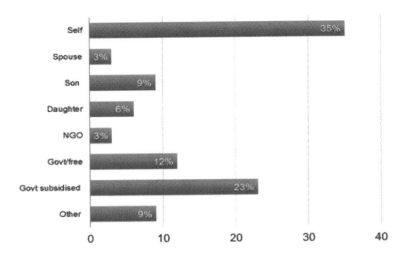

Figure 2.7 Who paid for the bulk of your medications?
Source: Own calculations from the survey
Note: n = 139

although it was unclear if the money they had used were given to them by their children or if they had used their own savings. That aside, it was also found that much fewer were dependent on their spouses (3 percent) to help pay for their medication compared with children, whether they be sons (9 percent) or daughters (6 percent). In this case, it is more likely that OPs would be more dependent on their children than spouses assuming that the former are still working.

The same pattern was found in the question on who paid for the most recent visit. While the majority (52 percent) said that they paid for the clinic or hospital bill, far fewer said that daughters covered the expenses (2 percent) compared with sons (6 percent), indicating that sons were more likely to undertake the financial responsibility of providing care towards the OP compared with daughters who presumably would undertake the actual physical caring for an elderly person (Figure 2.8).

On the question of an ideal healthcare system, the issue of healthcare costs frequently arose in the face-to-face interviews. Some felt that the high cost of healthcare has made it impossible for every OP to access quality healthcare equal for all. One woman said:

> I don't think all of us access the same quality of care . . . take for example those who can afford . . . they can go to a specialist in a private hospital instead of waiting for a specialist doctor in a public hospital . . . so there

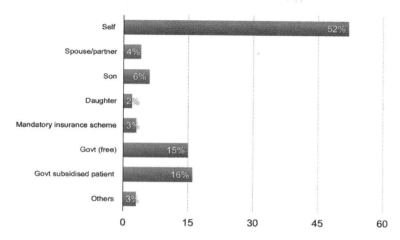

Figure 2.8 Who paid for most recent visit?
Source: Own calculations from the survey
Note: n = 103

is a built-in discrimination in the system . . . where the rich have more options.

> (IDI, Chinese Female, 67 years old)

A similar point was raised by another woman:

I don't think all have equal opportunity to good quality healthcare . . . there are people who cannot afford healthcare because they have some chronic disease . . . for Hari Raya, we visited some people at the rental flats . . . we saw one lady with chronic kidney disease . . . she cannot afford healthcare by herself and will have to rely on the government . . . here only the rich can afford . . . they have money . . . they can go to the private doctors and specialists . . . we have only one choice . . . although we know the service and care are better in the private hospitals.

> (IDI, Malay Female, 68 years old)

Some OPs provided candid remarks by saying that ideally they would like to see a healthcare system where costs are more heavily borne by the government rather than the individual or his or her family. One elderly man went to the extent of saying:

In my opinion, an ideal healthcare system is when no elderly should pay. . . . In other words, it would be free of charge not to burden the family . . . In this country, some people prefer to die than burden their family . . . this should not happen but it happens . . . like right now because I am a stroke patient, I am using my wife's Medisave . . . But what if she becomes sick . . . what if she runs out of Medisave . . . you need a solution for this . . . we are only gambling with our lives . . . we don't want to feel insecure in our old age . . . I do think about these things because I have come to this stage.

(IDI, Chinese Male, 73 years old)

Availability

As mentioned earlier, healthcare is easily available all over the country because Singapore is a city-state with a well-connected infrastructure and transport system. Moreover, there are a range of different healthcare providers available as well as different healthcare schemes an elderly person is eligible for in order to access timely and relevant healthcare. Among those surveyed, 96 percent said that they received healthcare when needed (Figure 2.9).

Acceptability

In terms of acceptability, the study found that the majority of respondents were satisfied with the quality of healthcare they received on their last visit. It was also found that the majority surveyed were satisfied with the healthcare services in terms of care and attention (70 percent), medical treatment (69 percent), and the availability of medicines (73 percent) (Figure 2.10).

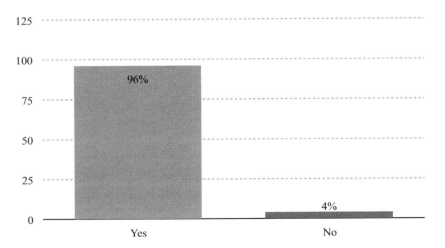

Figure 2.9 Received healthcare when needed?
Source: Own calculations from the survey
Note: n = 112

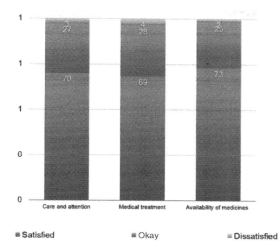

Figure 2.10 Overall satisfaction with the last visit to clinic

Source: Own calculations from the survey

Note: Care and attention, n = 110; Medical treatment, n = 109; Availability of medicines, n = 106

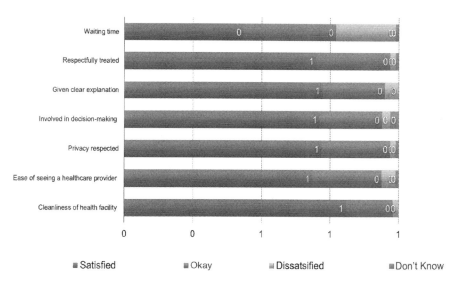

Figure 2.11 Rating of visit

Source: Own calculations from the survey

Note: n = 110

In spite of the overall respondent satisfaction of the healthcare system, the individuals interviewed were least satisfied with the waiting time and most satisfied with the cleanliness of the health facility (Figure 2.11). In fact, the most frequent complaint cited in the face-to-face interviews was waiting time, as exemplified in the following statement given by an older woman:

> I usually have to wait for an hour. . . . It is terrible. . . . That is too long. . . . Usually when my appointment is 10 am, I end up seeing the doctor at 11 am. . . . My husband will grumble that I have been away for so long . . . you call them first thing in the morning and yet I have to wait sometimes . . . I don't just turn up . . . before it was 2 hours, now it is much shorter but still I have to wait for a long time.
>
> (IDI, Chinese Female, 66 years old)

In spite of the waiting time being much longer in the public health facilities compared to the private clinics, one male respondent lauded the public healthcare system and said that it was superior to the services provided in the private clinics. In his opinion, his satisfaction of the services provided by the public healthcare system was bound up with the fact that the public healthcare facilities, which he most frequently uses, were able to provide most healthcare services unlike a private GP. In his words:

> They (the polyclinics) have everything compared to the private doctor . . . if I need a chest X-ray, I know I can get it straightaway at the polyclinic . . . if I go to the private clinic and if the doctors want me to get an X-ray, I have to go back to the polyclinic.
>
> (IDI, Malay Male, 63 years old)

Others associated their level of satisfaction with the trust they had formed in the healthcare system as well as in the health practitioners they have met. One respondent who is a kidney dialysis patient had this to say:

> At the dialysis centre I go to, the nurses are all very kind and nice to me . . . I trust them a lot . . . they are like family to me . . . they monitor my condition carefully . . . they are always there at my beck and call. . . . If I had to rate them, I would give them a ten upon ten.
>
> (IDI, Malay Male, 73 years old)

While the majority of respondents did not indicate a preference for doctors based on age or ethnicity (Figure 2.12 and Figure 2.13), the proportion of OPs who indicated that they had a preference for a doctor because of language was much higher. In this case, it is of no surprise that there are OPs who have indicated a preference for doctors whom they could communicate with (Figure 2.14).

When the respondents were asked if they found it easy to locate a healthcare provider one was happy with, the majority of respondents recorded satisfied (75 percent) or OK (28 percent) (Figure 2.15).

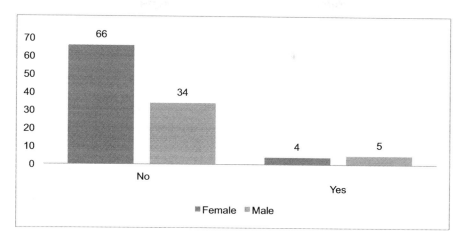

Figure 2.12 Doctor preference based on age
Source: Own calculations from the survey

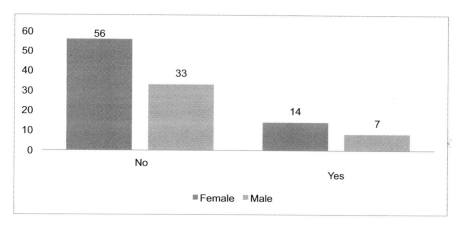

Figure 2.13 Doctor preference based on ethnicity
Source: Own calculations from the survey

In most polyclinics, patients see whichever general doctor is available. However, in a select few polyclinics, Family Physician (FP) Clinics have been set up. For patients seeing the doctors under the FP Clinics, their care is coordinated and managed by a designated senior doctor and his care team, allowing for

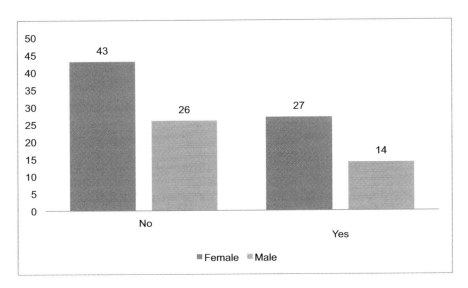

Figure 2.14 Doctor preference based on language
Source: Own calculations from the survey

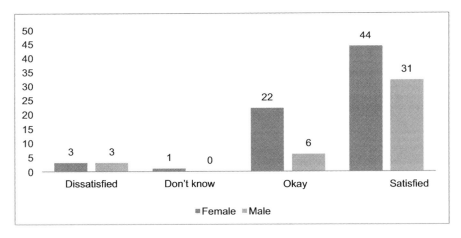

Figure 2.15 Ease of seeing healthcare provider one is happy with
Source: Own calculations from the survey

continuity of care and ensuring quality care for patients suffering from chronic diseases (National Healthcare Group Polyclinics 2016). In contrast to seeing a doctor in the general pool practising at the polyclinic that day, the consultation fees for seeing a doctor at the FP Clinic are much higher ranging from

Singapore $26 to $51.36 for Singaporeans, permanent residents and foreigners. An elderly woman said this of this care service:

> I go to Hougang Polyclinic because of the Family Physician Clinic . . . I like the idea of seeing the same doctor . . . it is like seeing a GP but the prices are lower because I get a subsidy because I come under the Pioneer Generation Package . . . for that reason, I don't mind going to Hougang Polyclinic although it is further from my house and I have to travel a longer distance.
>
> (IDI, Chinese, 66 years old)

In this case, the preference for doctor was not based on age, ethnicity or language but rather having someone whom the respondent has seen over years so that a rapport is built between the doctor and patient and the patient is confident about the medical advice he or she receives since the doctor is familiar with the patient's history.

2.5   Discussion and policy implications

In Singapore, no one is ever denied healthcare, including the elderly. To put it differently, the government has protected every citizen's and permanent resident's "right to health". This is achieved by having each individual take up a healthcare insurance plan such as in the case of the younger, working adults. The different healthcare schemes are designed in such a way that the individual takes care of his or her healthcare costs while a percentage of the costs are borne by the government. For those who are unable to afford purchasing a healthcare plan, as mentioned earlier, there is Medifund through which the individual's healthcare bills can be taken care of. Specifically, for the elderly, the right to health for this group has been achieved through the different number of health schemes targeted at meeting their needs in recent years given the growing elderly population, on the one hand, and the expansion of healthcare services as a whole, on the other. Moreover, there has been a range of subsidies to help older patients cover healthcare fees although it must be emphasised that by and large healthcare is never provided free. In this case, the elderly need to take responsibility for their own healthcare costs although the costs are subsidised depending on means-testing, albeit it must be said that the introduction of heavy subsidies in recent years has lightened the financial load off a substantial proportion of this group.

While Singapore's healthcare policies and the healthcare system enable access to relevant and appropriate healthcare in a timely fashion for all, including OPs, cost emerged as a critical factor in the narratives on the right to health and in turn, health security. All the respondents were well aware of the rising cost of healthcare in Singapore over the years and the anxiety felt by this group was evident in spite of the fact that the government had recently installed schemes such as the PGP which provides substantial subsidies. In fact, half of the respondents said that they were dependent on others, such as family members, financially, and yet they were found to pay for their own healthcare. This discrepancy may be explained by the fact that a large proportion of those surveyed received cash from their family members and out of the monies they received, they would set aside a certain sum to pay for their healthcare expenses. Budgeting for healthcare expenses is to be expected since the majority of the elderly have reported to be suffering from one or two illnesses at least.

In fact, not all illnesses are covered by the existing healthcare schemes, which calls in to question the protection of the rights of the elderly. Cancer is one such illness. In the report, "Salubris: Cancer in the Elderly – To Treat or Not to Treat?", it was documented that about 60 percent of malignant tumours inflict those in the age group 65 years and older. Moreover, OPs are 11 times more likely to develop a cancer than persons under the age of 65 (National Cancer Centre Singapore 2013). Particularly among the elderly poor who cannot afford health insurance, they are more likely not to be able to pay for cancer treatment. Among those who are diagnosed with first and second stage cancers, the out-of-pocket costs can be massive to the point where treatments become unaffordable and the OP refuses healthcare (Channel NewsAsia 2015).

While there appears to be no discrimination against any group of elderly within the larger group in accessing healthcare, there is a perception among some people that affordability influences the quality of healthcare an elderly person receives, thereby suggesting that access to quality care may be a privilege rather than a right in the country. This is especially true since the waiting time for specialist care in the public hospitals is much longer compared to if one were to approach private hospitals or clinics or utilise a specialist doctor at a public hospital as a private patient. Moreover, the quality of care received in public hospitals can vary considerably depending on the ward one is eligible to stay at.

Singapore's healthcare policy is predicated on the notion of "affordable healthcare for all". In reality, older people are struggling because of rising healthcare costs except for the fact that schemes such as the PGP were set up a few years back. The subsidies have been generally generous for elderly seeking outpatient care. However, because OPs are struggling to pay for dental care treatments and procedures, consideration should be given to ensuring that all OPs receive dental subsidies aside from PGP and CHAS beneficiaries since there are some groups such as CSC card holders who do not receive dental subsidies.

The other group that falls through the cracks is cancer patients who have to go on special treatment protocols on the long term. Currently, the bulk of healthcare schemes targeted at the elderly tend to mostly provide coverage for outpatient care for acute and minor illnesses as well as the management of chronic diseases. Because the current schemes tend not to cover chronic illnesses such as cancer, this leaves the elderly poor in particular, many of whom cannot afford health insurance plans, to avoid seeking timely and relevant treatment.

In terms of the "right to health awareness" related to raising levels of health education among OPs, it could be said that this been partially successful. While most OPs were well-informed about where to seek medical help, most respondents interviewed for the study were unsure, let alone "confused" as to which of the schemes they were eligible for and how healthcare subsidies kicked in for them at any one time. Based on the data collected in this study, the healthy seemed empowered but not the unhealthy as seen in the lack of health information held in the hands of the latter group. In this case, while the government has assumed agency on the part of OPs, that is, that they will seek out the health information they need, but in reality much more needs to be done to bring relevant information to this group so that they are sufficiently empowered.

Right to healthcare should also include the right to knowledge on the various policies and schemes available for OPs to access. Most elderly are uncertain as to which schemes they are eligible to access. The knowledge and information are important especially since the healthcare system operates on a co-payment arrangement where the elderly is expected to pay a portion of the final bill, however small it might be, after the subsidies have taken effect.

2.6   Concluding remarks

While Singapore is able to boast a healthcare system akin to that in any first world country, the healthcare system is not created on a rights-based approach. In other words, the healthcare system is not predicated on the assumption that the process of human development should be normatively based on international human rights standards and operationally directed to promoting and protecting human rights. This is only logical since the Singapore government has constantly reiterated that its perspective on rights is "pragmatic and non-ideological . . . even as it is fully committed to protecting the human rights of Singaporeans" (Yong 2015). It is not surprising then that the country lacks an institution/ body addressing human rights issues (e.g. a national human rights commission or ombudsperson) that looks into the health rights of OPs. In the same vein, it has no public health law or other relevant legislation that incorporates/ addresses the right to health, let alone fora or mechanisms aimed at promoting inter-sectoral action in the areas of health and human rights.

Where then are OPs in the discourse on health rights and health security? OPs are protected in so far as they are thought to be vulnerable since they have fewer savings compared with those in the working age cohorts and hence the government has recently enhanced its health policies and schemes in order to grant greater protections to OPs. If they do protect the rights of OPs, this only occurs to the extent that older people are never denied appropriate healthcare but are enabled to access appropriate health and social care although health and social care in old age are financed by individual out-of-pocket spending since the state does not support welfarism. The impact of such a policy is varied. Among older women, for example, who have held low levels of occupational status and possess limited social security protection, subsequently they have little choice but to rely on their children for support. And because current schemes tend not to provide total coverage for every older person thereby leaving many to be self-sufficient, it is doubtful if OP's rights to health are actually protected.

References

Agency for Integrated Care (2016) "Our Journey". URL: <www.aic.sg/about-us/more-about-aic> (accessed 20 July 2017).

Bloomberg (2015) "Lee Kuan Yew's Economic Miracle". 23 March. URL: <www.bloomberg.com/view/articles/2015-03-22/lee-kuan-yew-s-singapore-is-his-legacy> (accessed 17 July 2017).

Boh, Samantha (2016) "1 in 4 Singaporeans Aged Above 65 Developed Chronic Disease in Past Year: Study". The Straits Times, 11 November. URL: <www.straitstimes.com/singapore/one-in-four-singaporeans-aged-above-65-developed-chronic-disease-in-past-year-study> (accessed 9 January 2018).

Central Provident Fund (2017) "ElderShield". 30 June. URL: <www.cpf.gov.sg/members/schemes/schemes/healthcare/eldershield> (accessed 9 January 2018).

Chan, Angelique and Yap Mui Teng (2009) "Baby-Boomers Survey". Survey commissioned by the Ministry of Social and Family Development (MSF), Singapore. URL: < http://www.nas.gov.sg/archivesonline/data/pdfdoc/20090116004/baby_boomer_survey_7jan09.pdf > (accessed 9 January 2018).

Channel NewsAsia (2015) "The Cost of Cancer: Beyond the Treatment, a Financial Strain". URL: <www.channelnewsasia.com/news/health/the-cost-of-cancer-beyond-the-treatment-a-financial-strain-8235114> (accessed 9 January 2018).

CHAS (n.d.) "Administration of CHAS". URL: <https://www.chas.sg/gpcontent.aspx?id=454> (accessed 9 January 2018).

Chua, Lily A.V. (2009) "Personal Health Practices – Different Patterns in Males and Females". Statistics Singapore Newsletter, March. URL: < https://www.singstat.gov.sg/docs/default-source/default-document-library/publications/publications_and_papers/health/ssnmar09-pg12-16.pdf > (accessed 9 January 2018).

Department of Statistics (2009) *Population Trends*. Singapore: Department of Statistics.

—— (2014) *Population Trends 2014*. Singapore: Department of Statistics.

—— (2016) *General Household Survey 2015*. Singapore: Ministry of Trade & Industry. URL: <https://www.singstat.gov.sg/docs/default-source/default-document-library/publications/publications_and_papers/GHS/ghs2015/ghs2015.pdf> (accessed 9 January 2018).

—— (2017a) "Life Expectancy at Birth", 11 May. URL: <www.singstat.gov.sg/statistics/visualising-data/charts/life-expectancy-at-birth> (accessed 9 January 2018).

—— (2017b) "Population Trends", 27 September. URL: <www.singstat.gov.sg/statistics/visualising-data/storyboards/population-trends> (accessed 9 January 2018).

GBD 2015 DALYs and HALE Collaborators (2016) "Global, Regional, and National Disability-adjusted Life-years (DALYs) for 315 Diseases and Injuries and Healthy

Life Expectancy (HALE), 1990–2015: A Systematic Analysis for the Global Burden of Disease Study 2015". *Lancet*, 388: 1603–58.

Goh, Olivia (2006) "Successful Ageing – A Review of Singapore's Policy Approaches". Ethos, Issue 1. URL: <www.cscollege.gov.sg/Knowledge/Ethos/Issue%201%20 Oct%202006/Pages/Successful-Ageing-A-Review-of-Singapores-Policy-Approaches.aspx> (accessed 11 July 2017).

Government of Singapore (2018) "Pioneer Generation: Overview". 30 November. URL: < https://www.pioneers.sg/en-sg/Pages/Overview.aspx> (accessed 9 January 2018).

Income (2017) "Basic ElderShield 300 Premium Rates". URL: <www.income.com. sg/insurance/health-insurance/eldershield/details/basic-eldershield-300-premium-rates> (accessed 9 January 2018).

Jones, Gavin. (1995) "Population and the Family in Southeast Asia", *Journal of Southeast Asian Studies* 26(1): 184–95.

——— (2009) "Women, Marriage and Family in Southeast Asia". In *Gender Trends in Southeast Asia: Women Now, Women in the Future*, edited by Theresa W. Devasahayam. Singapore: Institute of Southeast Asian Studies.

Jones, Gavin, Straughan, Pauline T. and Angelique Chan (2009) "Very Low Fertility in Pacific Asian Countries". In *Ultra-low Fertility in Pacific Asia: Trends, Causes and Policy Issues*, edited by Gavin Jones, Pauline T. Straughan and Angelique Chan. New York: Routledge.

Kang, Soon Hock, Tan, Ern Ser and Yap Mui Teng (2013) *National Survey of Senior Citizens 2011*. Singapore: Institute of Policy Studies.

Koh, Benedict S.K., Mitchell, Olivia S., Tanuwidjaja, Toto and Joelle Fong (2008) "Investment Patterns in Singapore's Central Provident Fund System". *Journal of Pension Economics and Finance*, 7: 37–65.

Kotwani, Monica (2017) "Caring for an Ageing Society: How to Ensure Singapore Has Enough Nurses". Channel NewsAsia, 10 June. URL: <www.channelnewsasia. com/news/singapore/caring-for-an-ageing-society-how-to-ensure-singapore-has-enough-8921492> (accessed 9 January 2018).

Lee, Amanda (2014) "Silver Support Scheme to Assist Needy Seniors With Annual Payouts". 18 August. URL: <www.todayonline.com/singapore/silver-support-scheme-assist-needy-seniors-annual-payouts> (accessed 18 January 2018).

Mehta, Kalyani (2002) "Gender and Cultural Dynamics of Retirement". In *Extending Frontiers: Social Issues and Social Work in Singapore*, edited by Ngoh Tiong Tan and Kalyani Mehta. Singapore: Eastern Universities Press.

Ministry of Health (2013) "Singapore Healthcare System". 30 October. URL: <www.moh.gov.sg/content/moh_web/home/our_healthcare_system.html> (accessed 20 July 2017).

——— (2014a) *Singapore Burden of Disease Study 2010*. Singapore: Epidemiology & Disease Control Division, Ministry of Health.

——— (2014b) "Government Health Expenditure and Healthcare Financing". URL: <www.moh.gov.sg/content/moh_web/home/statistics/Health_Facts_Singapore/ Healthcare_Financing.html> (accessed 1 September 2014).

——— (2015a) "Medisave for Chronic Disease Management Programme (CDMP) and Vaccinations". 13 March. URL: <www.moh.gov.sg/content/moh_web/ home/policies-and-issues/elderly_healthcare.html> (accessed 9 January 2018).

——— (2015b) "MediShield Life Coverage for All Singapore Residents to start on 1 November 2015". 2 August. URL: < https://www.moh.gov.sg/content/

moh_web/home/pressRoom/pressRoomItemRelease/2015/medishield-life-coverage-for-all-singapore-residents-to-start-on.html> (accessed 9 January 2018).

———— (2016) "Medisave Uses and Withdrawal Limits". 1 July. URL: <www.moh.gov.sg/content/moh_web/home/costs_and_financing/schemes_subsidies/medisave/Withdrawal_Limits.html> (accessed 18 July 2017).

———— (2017a) "Costs and Financing". 7 September. URL: <www.moh.gov.sg/content/moh_web/home/costs_and_financing.html> (accessed 9 January 2018).

———— (2017b) "Government Health Expenditure and Healthcare Financing". 27 September. URL: <www.moh.gov.sg/content/moh_web/home/statistics/Health_Facts_Singapore/Healthcare_Financing.html> (accessed 9 January 2018).

———— (2017c) "Number of Policyholders for MediShield and Integrated Shield Plans, Annual". 6 February. URL: <https://data.gov.sg/dataset/medishield-and-integrated-shield-plans?resource_id=dfd1bf2a-4277-4cc3-8ece-483531c730f0> (accessed 9 January 2018).

———— (2017d) "Pioneer Generation Package". 25 May. URL: <www.moh.gov.sg/content/moh_web/home/costs_and_financing/schemes_subsidies/pioneer-generation-package.html> (accessed 8 January 2018).

Ministry of Manpower (2017a) "Retirement and Re-employment Act". 30 November. URL: http://www.mom.gov.sg/employment-practices/employment-rights-conditions/retirement/Pages/retirement.aspx (accessed 9 January 2018).

———— (2017b) "What Is the Central Provident Fund (CPF)". 3 October. URL: <www.mom.gov.sg/employment-practices/central-provident-fund/what-is-cpf> (accessed 9 January 2018).

———— (2017c) "Responsible Re-employment". 20 December 2017. URL: <http://www.mom.gov.sg/employment-practices/re-employment/responsible-re-employment> (accessed 9 January 2018).

Ministry of Social and Family Development (2014) "Ageing Families in Singapore". Insight Series Paper 02/2015. Singapore: Strategic Planning, Research and Development Division, Ministry of Social and Family Development.

National Cancer Centre Singapore (2013) *Salubris: Cancer in the Elderly – To Treat or Not to Treat?* Singapore: National Cancer Centre.

National Healthcare Group Polyclinics (2016) "FAQs on Family Physician(FP) Clinic". URL: <www.nhgp.com.sg/faq.aspx?id=a85ce30b4d954c1298e4c0df0faaedeb> (accessed 21 July 2017).

Neo Chai Chin (2014) "450,000 Eligible for Pioneer Generation Package". Today, 9 February. URL: <www.todayonline.com/singapore/450000-eligible-pioneer-generation-package> (accessed 9 January 2018).

Reisman, David (2009) *Social Policy in an Ageing Society: Age and Health in Singapore.* Cheltenham: Edward Elgar.

Report on the State of the Elderly in Singapore (2008/2009). "Release 1: Trends in Population Ageing: Profile of Singapore's Elderly Population". URL:<https://www.moh.gov.sg/content/dam/moh_web/Publications/Reports/2009/1/State%20of%20the%20Elderly_Release%201.pdf> (accessed 9 January 2018).

Tan Teck Boon (2015) "A Super-aged Singapore: Policy Implications for a Smart Nation". RSIS Commentary, No. 193, 10 September. URL: <www.rsis.edu.sg/rsis-publication/rsis/co15193-a-super-aged-singapore-policy-implications-for-a-smart-nation/#.WWxJdulLdPY> (accessed 9 January 2018).

United Nations, Department of Economic and Social Affairs, Population Division (2015) World Population Prospects 2015 – Data Booklet (ST/ESA/ SER.A/377).

URL: <https://esa.un.org/unpd/wpp/publications/Files/WPP2015_DataBooklet.pdf> (accessed 9 January 2018).

Wai, Desmond (2016) "The Low-Down on Rising Medical Costs". Today, 17 November. URL: <www.todayonline.com/singapore/low-down-rising-medical-costs> (accessed 9 January 2018).

Wu, Treena and Angelique Chan (2011) "Older Women, Health, and Social Care in Singapore". *Asia Europe Journal*, 8: 513–26.

Yong, Clarissa (2015) "Singapore's Approach to Human Rights 'Pragmatic', Says Govt in Report to the United Nations". The Straits Times, 11 December. URL: <www.straitstimes.com/singapore/singapores-approach-to-human-rights-pragmatic-says-govt-in-report-to-the-united-nations> (accessed 9 January 2018).

Zhang Wei, Heng Chye Kiang and Fung John Chye (2017) "Community Planning Framework of Community Care for the Elderly in Singapore". Paper presented at 14th International Congress of Asian Planning Schools Association, Tsinghua University, Beijing China.

3 Malaysia

How Kee Ling, Zamri Hassan,
Faizah Mas'ud and Sidiah John Siop

3.1 Introduction

Malaysia is experiencing population ageing at an accelerated pace. According to the latest population estimate of 32,049.70 million, older persons (OPs) 60 years and above constitute 8.3 percent of the total population (Department of Statistics 2017). According to projections by the United Nations, by 2020, the proportion of the OPs 60 years and above will be 9.9 percent and by 2030, OPs will constitute 15 percent of the total population; by 2050, the proportion of OPs will further increase to 20.4 percent (United Nations Department of Economic and Social Affairs – UNDESA 2015).

Is Malaysia ready to meet the needs of its growing ageing population? While families are still the primary care providers for OPs in Malaysia, changing family structure and declining family support has signalled the needs for a systematic social protection programme to be in place to ensure that the needs and rights of OPs are met. In recent years, the periodical news of incidents of abuse and neglect of OPs in both residential care and in the community in the mass media may well reflect the tip of the iceberg. Attention has now turned to the need for the formulation of a legislative framework to protect the basic human rights of OPs (Siti Zaharah Jamaluddin et al. 2017; Human Rights Commission of Malaysia 2015). However, it needs to be stressed that when referring to elder rights, the concern goes beyond the protection against abuse and neglect, but a whole range of rights including rights to income security, and rights to work (if one wishes) and rights to healthcare. It is in this context that this chapter explores the health rights of OPs in Malaysia, specifically the experiences of OPs in accessing and financing healthcare, and the extent to which public policies enable OPs to have health security.

3.2 Health status of older people in Malaysia

There is a dearth of nationwide surveys specifically on the health condition of OPs; however, the Ministry of Health conducts a national health and morbidity survey every five years across the population to monitor the health of the population in Malaysia (www.iku.gov.my). Although studies on the health status of

OPs are limited, previous studies in the last three decades have provided a picture of the health status and health-seeking behaviour of older Malaysians.

An earlier study sponsored by the World Health Organization (WHO) in Peninsula Malaysia in 1984/85 (Chen Andrews, Josef, Chan and Arokiasamy 1986) with a purposive sample of 1,000 OPs found that 72 percent reported themselves as healthy, but all of them reported specific health problems and half of them took prescribed medication. Common problems included poor eye-sight and problems with chewing and hearing. The use of over-the-counter medication was reported by 29 percent, while the use of traditional medication was reported by 21 percent of the respondents.

A study by Ong and Wong (2002, as cited in Ong 2009) on OPs in the capital city of Kuala Lumpur and the satellite town of Petaling Jaya found the majority could still function well in activities of daily living (ADLs). In terms of self-assessment of health status, 35.6 percent rated their health as good, 52.9 percent rated it average and 11.6 percent reported poor health. However, about 60 percent reported having chronic health problems, with the most common being high blood pressure and arthritis.

A nationwide study conducted in 2008 on mental health and quality of life of older Malaysians (MHQoLOM) involving 2,980 OPs is probably one of the most comprehensive surveys in the last two decades (Siop 2008; Siop, Verbrugge and Tengku Aizan 2008). The study employed a multi-stage proportional stratified sampling procedure taking into account the absolute number of OPs in an enumeration block by state. The population in the study consisted of older Malaysians aged 60 years and above who reside in the community throughout the thirteen states in Malaysia; Johore, Kedah, Kelantan, Melaka, Negeri Sembilan, Pahang, Perak, Perlis, Pulau Pinang, Selangor, Terengganu, Sabah and Sarawak, including the Federal Territory of Kuala Lumpur. The findings from this study revealed that the most common medical conditions or diseases were arthritis (41.4 percent), hypertension (30.5 percent), diabetes mellitus (14.4 percent), circulatory disorders (11.8 percent) and memory problems (10.4 percent). The OPs reported a mean of 1.6 (S.D ±1.63) for medical conditions, with 72 percent reporting at least one disease. Arthritis, hypertension, memory problems, eye disorders and gastrointestinal disorders were more common among women than men. By contrast, men were more likely to have reported heart diseases, respiratory disorders and renal disorders. Despite the medical problems, more than two-thirds of the respondents rated their health as "good" and "excellent". About 38 percent of the respondents rated their health as "very poor" and "poor". Men were more likely to rate their health as "good" and "excellent" (65.0 percent for men versus 59.7 percent for women), whereas slightly more women rated their health as "poor" and "very poor" (40.2 percent for women versus 35.0 percent for men).

A cross-sectional study on the health needs of OPs aged 60 years and above (n = 77) in a semi-urban village in Sarawak, Malaysia (Siop 2003) which employed a universal sampling method revealed that a high proportion of the respondents had health problems. A large proportion of the OPs had cramping/pain in their extremities (43 percent), 25 percent had varicosities, 22 percent had high blood pressure and 3 percent had oedema. A fairly high proportion of the elderly had problems with vision (58 percent), while 33 percent reported hearing problems, 39 percent had dental problems and 31 percent were suffering from cognitive impairment. Problems of neuromusculoskeletal function were also reported; 36 percent had joint pain, 36 percent had back/shoulder/neck pain and 14 percent had gait/ambulation disturbances. Surprisingly, only 3 percent had urinary incontinence.

A study among OPs in residential care homes in Peninsular Malaysia (Zaiton, Nor Afiah and Latiffah 2006) found that chronic illnesses were a significant predictor for functional dependence. Chronic illness is defined as any self-reported diseases such as diabetes mellitus, hypertension, ischemic heart disease, respiratory problem (chronic obstructive pulmonary disease and asthma), osteoarthritis and gout.

Another study worthy of mention is one which examined physical as well as mental health problems among OPs in a rural community in Sepang, Selangor conducted by Sherina Mohd Sidik, Rampal and Afifi (2004). With a sample of 223 respondents with a mean age of 69.7 years, the study found that the prevalence of physical health problems such as chronic illness and functional dependence were 60.1 percent and 15.7 percent, respectively, while the prevalence of mental health problems such as depression and cognitive impairment were 7.6 percent and 22.4 percent, respectively.

A study by Ng, Tengku-Aizan and Tey (2011) examined the perceived health status of OPs and its association with social participation. The study found that OPs with good perceived health status reported more varieties of daily activity participation and tended to engage in paid work only or with leisure activities whereas those who perceived to have poor health were more likely to engage in leisure activities only or leisure and family role activities.

A more recent study conducted by Wan Ibrahim and Zainab (2014) among 214 OPs in Kelantan, a rural region in Peninsular Malaysia, found that "not many respondents are suffering from chronic diseases that require ongoing medical treatment". However, the common illnesses reported were hypertension (25.2 percent), followed by asthma (19.2 percent) and a smaller percentage suffered from diabetes (3.5 percent), heart failure (2.6 percent), renal failure (2.6 percent), tuberculosis (1.7 percent) and co-morbidity diabetes and hypertension (1.7 percent).

3.3   Health system and policies focusing on older persons

Malaysia has a long established public healthcare system providing universal access to a comprehensive package of healthcare services. However, since the mid-1980s, in line with the new directions in economic policy, and fuelled by rising incomes and urbanisation, there has been a transformation of the public health system towards corporatisation and privatisation. This contributed to a proliferation of private hospitals in the past few decades, as well as the manifold increase in private specialist services (Chee and Barraclough 2009). However, hospital care is still heavily dominated by the public sector i.e. Ministry of Health being the largest healthcare provider. Approximately 75 percent of all hospital beds and 71 percent of the total hospital admissions were reported in the public sector (Lim, Sivasampu, AriZa and Nabilah 2011).

In terms of healthcare facilities provision, for the year 2013–2014 there was a total of 355 hospitals that provided acute care services with a density of 0.12 hospitals per 10,000 population. The majority of the hospitals and beds in Malaysia are concentrated in the State of Selangor & Federal Territories of Putrajaya and Kuala Lumpur, and in major cities and towns (Ministry of Health, Annual Report 2014).

Malaysia has begun to recognise the trend towards population ageing in the last three decades. There have been two policies of significance over the last two decades: first, the National Policy for the Elderly (NPE) in 1995, revised in 2011; and second, the National Health Policy 2008. Tengku Aizan and Nurizan (2008) traced the development of NPE to the Declaration of Rights and Responsibilities of Older Persons by the International Federation on Ageing; and the formation of the 18 United Nations Principles for Older Persons in December 1991, commonly known as Resolution 46/91, as a catalyst for NPE. Pursuant to this, the Ministry of Health developed the National Plan of Action for Health Care of Older Persons in 1997.

Consequently, in 2008 the National Health Policy for Older Persons was formulated with the view of the need for a more effective, coordinated and comprehensive healthcare system. Six guiding principles were outlined in the formulation of the policy: (a) maintaining autonomy and self -reliance; (b) recognising the distinctive needs of OPs; (c) supporting carers; (d) promoting healthy ageing; (e) providing continuity of care; and (f) maintaining the rights of OPs to quality of life and death. The policy was to achieve four major objectives:

1   to improve the health status of OPs;
2   to encourage participation in health promotion and disease prevention activities throughout the life course;
3   to provide age friendly, affordable, equitable, accessible, culturally acceptable, gender sensitive and seamless healthcare services in a holistic manner at all levels; and
4   to advocate and support the development of an enabling environment for independent living.

Although the policy does not clearly speak to the language of rights, the concept of rights is embedded in objectives 3 and 4. In addition, the policy was implemented based on seven strategies which are: (a) health promotion, (b) provision of a continuum of comprehensive healthcare services, (c) human resources planning and development, (d) information system, (e) research and development, (f) interagency and intersectoral collaboration, and (g) legislation. This last strategy on legislation explicitly states to "advocate the development of new legislation and review existing ones, to ensure the preservation of the dignity and autonomy of older persons, the quality and standards of service provision, promote health, prevent age discrimination and abuse of older persons" (National Health Policy for Older Persons 2008: 15).

Several guidelines were also established to provide the framework for service delivery. These guidelines are the clinical practice guidelines on management of dementia in 2003, which was updated in 2009 (Ministry of Health 2009), and the guidelines on oral healthcare for the elderly in Malaysia (Ministry of Health 2002). The latest initiative is the Elder Healthcare Act to ensure that quality care has been put in motion (Tengku Aizan 2015).

The government's commitments to the health of OPs are translated into various activities conducted at the health centres, which include health promotion and education; health screening and assessment; medical examination, counselling, treatment and referral; home visits and home care; rehabilitation; and social recreation and welfare. The recreational, social and welfare activities are being carried out by the communities and the OPs who live within the operational area of the health centres. The main purpose of these activities is to facilitate community participation in order to attain healthy and active ageing. In 2013, 239 health centres in Malaysia have formed the "Elderly Club" that run the recreational, social and welfare activities (Country Report 2013). All the healthcare service activities for the elderly are coordinated at the state level.

At the government hospitals, services provided are acute medical care, long-term care, discharge plan, psycho geriatric care, physiotherapy, occupational therapy, clinical pharmacy, counselling and medico-social/welfare. A significant feature of medical care for the OPs adopted by the hospitals in Malaysia is the multi-disciplinary approach considering the multiple problems usually faced by OPs. Nine government hospitals have geriatric units/wards. There are sixteen geriatricians (five with the Ministry of Health, four with universities and seven with private hospitals); nine psycho-geriatricians (six with Ministry of Health and three with universities); and four family medicine specialists in community geriatric and four medical gerontologists. From 1996 to 2013, 300 nurses and assistant medical officers had attended six months of post-basic training in geriatric nursing. All government primary healthcare facilities provide healthcare services to the elderly. The government clinics and hospitals are made "elderly friendly" by giving the OPs priority in waiting lines. Pensioners are eligible for free treatment and hospital fees are waived for the poor elderly (Country Report 2013).

3.4 Assessing health security among older persons in Malaysia

3.4.1 Assessment methods

In order to assess the health rights of OPs in Malaysia, a quantitative survey questionnaire and qualitative methods were developed for this study.

Three research sites were chosen for the purpose of ensuring that variation of experiences as a result of socioeconomic backgrounds, ethnicity and linguistic issues as well as urban and rural disparities, can be captured. The three sites are: (a) The capital city Kuala Lumpur and the State of Selangor, (b) Terengganu in the east coast of Peninsular Malaysia, and (c) Sarawak in Borneo (also referred to as East Malaysia together with Sabah).

A stratified sampling method was used to ensure that about equal number of men and women, urban and rural, various ethnicity and different economic and occupational backgrounds are represented. A conscious attempt was also made to ensure that the three age cohorts, that is young old (60–69 years old), middle old (70–79 years old) and the oldest old were represented in the quantitative survey proportionately – 60 percent young old, 30 percent middle old and 10 percent oldest old.

Both quantitative survey and qualitative interviews were conducted face-to-face and as much as possible in the language of the respondents. In cases where the researchers were not able to converse in the language of the respondents, interpreters acting as research assistants were used. Qualitative interviews were conducted either using In-Depth Interviews (IDIs) or Focus Group Discussions (FGDs). These FGDs were conducted with either members of Older Persons' Organisations or groups of OPs according to language or ethnic backgrounds, by geographical location or by gender. Apart from Bahasa Melayu (the official language of Malaysia), local Malay dialects, Tamil, Mandarin, English, Iban, Bidayuh and Melanau were used in the study. All interviews were transcribed, and those in other languages were translated into English. In the process of translation, efforts were made to retain the original meaning of the statements.

The survey covered 300 participants, and the qualitative interviews involved twenty IDIs and four FGDs. Although the number of participants is small, and no claim is made for the findings to be representative of the larger older population, it has nevertheless yielded insightful data, highlighting salient issues and concerns for policy implications.

3.4.2 Key findings

The study found that of the 300 respondents participating in the study, 77.1 percent (229 participants) were sick/injured in the last twelve months. Slightly more female participants (39.4 percent) were sick or injured and need healthcare in the past twelve months than male participants (37.7 percent) out of the 229 participants. Table 3.1 shows the percentage of OPs who reported minor health ailments in the month preceding the survey.

Table 3.1 Percentage distribution of minor health ailments reported by participants

Minor health ailments	percent (n = 300)
Coughing	51
Headache	49.3
Joints pain	47.7
Back or hip pain	41.3
Feeling weak	38.7
Shoulder pain	31.3
Dizziness	31
Fever	28.7
Chest pain	14.3
Breathing problem	12.7
Trembling hand	11
Stomach ache	10
Skin problem	7.3
Diarrhoea	7.3
Constipation	6
Loss of bladder control	5.7
Vomiting	5.7
Loss of bowel control	3.3

Source: Own calculations from the survey

On the question if they have been diagnosed with any diseases, a similar trend as in previous studies cited above were found. Table 3.2 shows the percentage who reported to have been diagnosed with the following common diseases. The findings showed that hypertension is most common in the list of diseases, followed by diabetes and arthritis, whereas gastritis or ulcer, cardiovascular diseases, cataract and respiratory disorders are also among the higher groups of diseases. Of concern is that 4 percent were diagnosed with depression, 2 percent dementia and another 2 percent with "folk illnesses", presumably some undiagnosed mental health-related issues.

Accessibility

The majority of respondents (77 percent) has accessed healthcare facilities in the last twelve months. The use of the healthcare was mainly because they were unwell or injured. More than 35 percent have gone through various illnesses and injuries in the past twelve months. 72.7 percent of the participants have been regularly taking medicines during the last twelve months. 34 percent of the participants have been taking medicines for high blood pressure or hypertension, followed by diabetes (13.3 percent), cardiovascular disease or heart

Table 3.2 Percentage distribution of common diseases

Common diseases	percent (n = 300)
Hypertension	51
Diabetes	26.3
Arthritis	26.3
Gastritis or ulcer	11.7
Cardiovascular diseases	11.3
Cataract	11
Asthma, Emphysema or Bronchitis	10.3
Cancer	4
Depression	4
Stroke	3.7
Chronic kidney disease	3.3
Dementia	2
Thyroid problem	2
Incontinence	1.7
Obesity	1.7
Anaemia	1
Others (Folk illness, culturally bound syndrome)	2

Source: Own calculations from the survey

attack (5.3 percent), gastric (2.7 percent) and asthma (2.3 percent). 82.2 percent of those who were sick did receive healthcare while 17.2 percent did not. The reasons given for them not getting healthcare were because of 'self-treatment' (58.1 percent), afraid to have treatment (7.5 percent), not enough money to pay for treatment (4.3 percent), no transportation available (4.3 percent) and 1.1 percent reported not having enough money for transportation.

FGDs with a group of rural women found that some of them had never been to any health facilities for treatment. An older woman said:

No, I don't have any treatment. I only pray by myself. Ya Allah.
(FGD, older woman, 82 years old, rural Sarawak)

When asked why she did not want to access treatment, she said:

I don't know how to eat pills. We *orang tua* (old people) are all like that. If I have stomach ache, and my family said: ma'am, ma'am, this is for you to eat (acting as if someone giving a tablet) I don't want to eat them, I'm afraid I'll get intoxicated and die. I'm wondering myself, why I don't want to go? I have sickness. My eyes are not clear anymore. Even my ears can't listen well.

Outpatient care in the study refers to respondents' experience in the latest visit and included healthcare received at a hospital, health centre or clinic and may include visits by healthcare workers. In terms of geographical accessibility, the findings indicated that most of the 'place of healthcare provider or facility' was located in their own town (73.2 percent), while 8.4 percent in other cities or towns. 7.6 percent of the OPs in the study used a healthcare provider or facility located in the same village, while for 0.8 percent of the respondents, the healthcare provider or facility was located in another village.

Although the location of the facility they used was found in the same area where they live, the condition of the road and the required transportation influenced the level of accessibility. With the lack of good public transportation in Malaysia, ownership of a private vehicle either by the OPs themselves or family members afforded them the ease to access these facilities. The findings showed that almost 71.2 percent of the respondents reached the healthcare facilities by private vehicles in their last visit, followed by 18.5 percent who used public transportation. 4.1 percent used a cab, 1.1 percent walked to the clinic during their last visit and 0.4 percent used a bicycle. The remaining 4.7 percent used other means.

One obvious case example applied to the indigenous community of *Orang Asli* in Peninsular Malaysia. With the improvement of the road, they reported to access the healthcare facilities more easily.

> Now, the road is improved. If I want to go to the nearest town[1] (where the good clinic located), I also can. In the past, we were getting help from flying doctor. Sometimes heli came to fetch us, depending on the health condition, if serious, heli will come within half an hour especially those who were having problems with pregnancy. A group of medical health people will come from the town.
>
> (IDI, older man, 60 years old)

Similarly, time taken to get to the clinic is another indicator of accessibility. The findings showed that 40.4 percent of the respondents took between sixteen to thirty minutes to travel to a health facility, while 1.9 percent took more than sixty-one minutes and more to travel to the clinic; in contrast among those who spent much less time travelling to the nearest health facility, nearly 33.6 percent spent between one to fifteen minutes while 18.9 percent took thirty-one to forty-five minutes.

Access to outpatient care may also be dependent on whether the OP has the autonomy to decide if they should seek medical care or not. To the question, "who in your family made the decision about going to health facilities?", the findings indicated that the decision was not always made by the OPs themselves. While slightly over half of the OPs, i.e. 61.6 percent made the decision themselves about receiving treatment, 23.2 percent had decisions made for them by their son or daughter, while another 14 percent by their spouse or partner. In contrast, 0.7 percent had non-family members and 0.4 percent had other family members make the decision for them.

Inpatient care refers to experiences of overnight stay in a hospital or healthcare facility within the last three years. The study found that 32.6 percent of the participants stayed overnight in a health facility in the last three years. Out of this, 66.4 percent stayed overnight in a district or public hospital, 17 percent at a private hospital, and 16 percent stayed at a township or District Hospital. Similar to accessing outpatient care, the most common mode of transportation used was by private vehicle (81.6 percent); 7 percent were taken there by ambulance; 6.1 percent got there by public transport; and 5.3 percent by taxi. Compared with outpatient care, the time taken to reach the health facility is longer. About 15 percent took fifteen minutes and less (while 33.6 percent for outpatient); 49.5 percent needed fifteen to thirty minutes (while 40.4 percent for outpatient); 21.5 percent less than forty-five minutes (while 18.9 percent for outpatient); 9.3 percent more than forty-five minutes but within an hour, while 4.7 percent took more than an hour (while 1.9 percent for outpatient care).

The findings show that health facilities for hospitalisation are further away from the place of residence of OPs. Compared with accessing outpatient care, accessing inpatient care is influenced by not just distance but also if they were able to get to the health facility. More than 90 percent of the respondents reported that they needed someone to bring them or stay with them in the hospital. Furthermore, for those from the lower income group, it may mean that the family members who take them there may have to lose their pay days. Daily paid workers or farmers, who form a sizeable group in the lower income strata, are those who are in this position. The findings showed that 37.4 percent of the respondents' family members did lose their working days, and out of this, 81.3 percent of the respondents' family members lost around one to five working days, while 2.1 percent of them lost eleven working days and more, indicating that there are relatives who have to stay away from the job to be with the OPs, a point very much related to the issue of affordability as well.

Affordability

Affordability refers to the healthcare facilities with a standard that can be securely attained by OPs without unreasonable burden on their household income. According to Evan, Hsu and Boerma (2013), financial affordability is a measure of people's ability to pay for services without financial hardship. It takes into account not only the price of the health services but also indirect and opportunity costs (e.g., the costs of transportation to and from facilities and of taking time away from work). Affordability is influenced by the wider health financing system and by household income.

OUTPATIENT CARE

Figure 3.1 shows the percentage of respondents paying various fees to access outpatient healthcare. Majority of the respondents, that is, 86.1 percent did not spend any money for the last visit on healthcare provider's fee, while 13.2 percent spent RM 1 to RM 500. However, 0.4 percent spent RM1501 to RM 2000 for their last visit, and another 0.4 percent spent RM 2001 and above. This reflects that OPs did take advantage of the almost free outpatient treatment available in government hospitals and clinics.

For medicine, most of the respondents did not spend any money for their last visit (79.9 percent), whereas 19.8 percent of the respondents spent RM 1 to RM 500 on medicines for their last visit. The majority of the respondents (97.8 percent) did not spend any money on tests for their last visit. However, 1.8 percent of the respondents spent RM1 to RM500 on tests while 0.4 percent of them spent RM1501 to RM2000 on tests on their last visit.

However, while outpatient treatment may be inexpensive, OPs who are not residing near a clinic, particularly those residing in rural or remote areas, have to spend money on transportation. The figure showed that 51.3 percent of the respondents spent RM1 to RM500 on transport for their last visit, while 48.7 percent of them did not spend any money on transport on their last visit.

As to who finances the cost of accessing healthcare, the findings showed that 19 percent of the OPs in the sample paid for themselves, 28.6 percent had the fee paid by their sons while another 19 percent had the fee paid by daughters, 16.7 percent by spouses or partners, and 10.7 percent by the government.

Overall for outpatient care, the figure suggests that OPs were able to benefit from the almost free treatment provided by government clinics, and if they did have to pay, the cost is within the capacity of the OPs or their families. For inpatient care, the findings are different.

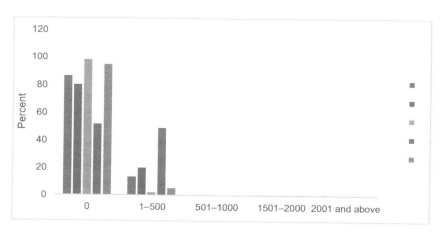

Figure 3.1 Payment of various outpatient healthcare fees
Source: Own calculations from the survey

INPATIENT CARE

Inpatient care or hospitalisation in Malaysia is mainly provided by public or general hospitals in selected town centres, especially in the district and state's capital. In the last three decades, private hospitals are burgeoning in the major cities in the different states of Malaysia. This means rural elders would have to travel a distance and be away from the families when they require inpatient care. The inpatient cost varies greatly between government and private healthcare facilities in fees. Figure 3.2 reflects the affordability of inpatient healthcare facilities to older Malaysians. Hospitalisation cost is almost nothing as more than 90 percent did not have to pay anything for the medicines, tests and other procedures. The payment incurred includes the fees which are around RM1- RM500. 12.5 percent of the respondents paid more than RM2001 for the fees which may reflect the type of provider they used, in this case most likely private. The other cost incurred is for transportation. 31.8 percent had to pay RM500 and below for a return trip to the hospital.

As to who paid for the cost associated with hospitalisation, 47.1 percent of the OPs in the study paid for themselves, followed by the government (36.4 percent), their son (7 percent), their daughter (4 percent) and their spouse or partner (2.9 percent), while 0.4 percent relied on other family members and other people. Findings in relation to who accompanied them to the hospital found that 71.5 percent of the respondents had someone accompany them for the visit, while 28.5 percent accessed the health facility themselves. On loss of pay because of accompanying a relative to the health facility, 77.6 percent of the respondents' family members did not have any loss of pay while 20.9 percent of them did lose a total of RM1 to RM500. For those who did not know their total loss of pay, there were only 1.5 percent of them.

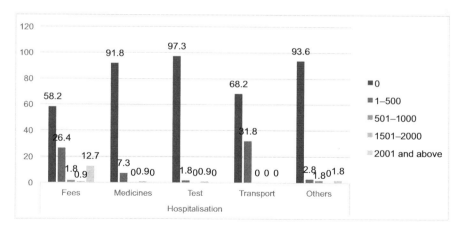

Figure 3.2 Payment of various hospital care costs

Source: Own calculations from the survey

Availability

As mentioned in the earlier sections, healthcare is easily available for those who live in the urban centres, have private transport, and have the means to choose from the range of public and private care facilities. For OPs from rural areas and who are often economically less able to choose private healthcare, government clinics are located within the vicinity of the OPs' villages. As mentioned by a senior health official in one FGD, "every ten kilometres, there is a clinic". For those living in remote areas, they have access to healthcare since healthcare providers visit their villages once a month through a mobile service.

AVAILABILITY OF MEDICINE

Medication for chronic diseases such as diabetics and hypertension – often associated with old age – are also easily available and provided free for OPs. However, FGD with *Orang Asli* men found that this is not the case.

> It just that sometimes the medicines that we have been prescribed is not available. So, I do not go to the health clinic either. If the nurse said the medicine is available, then I will go visit the health centre.

Another man said:

> Because the road is getting better, at the moment I sell my durian or *petai* (bitter beans) outside this village, then I will take the opportunity to visit the hospital or clinic at the nearest town to get the medicines.

FGDs with senior ex-health officials revealed that one could even request for medication to be posted, provided that the OP live within the postal service areas. This service makes it convenient for many OPs, especially those living in the major towns.

Acceptability

Acceptability is important to ensure OPs are able to access healthcare and fully utilise available facilities according to their needs. Health providers need not only provide affordable services but need to be respectful and sensitive to their personal preference, especially based on culture and patient needs (Dillip et al. 2012). Acceptability is low for two reasons: when patients perceive services to be ineffective or when social and cultural factors such as language or the age, sex, ethnicity or religion of the health provider discourages them from seeking services (Evans, Hsu and Boerma 2013).

OUTPATIENT CARE

On the question of satisfaction of healthcare facilities, a question was asked about which health facilities the participants most often visited in case of an illness

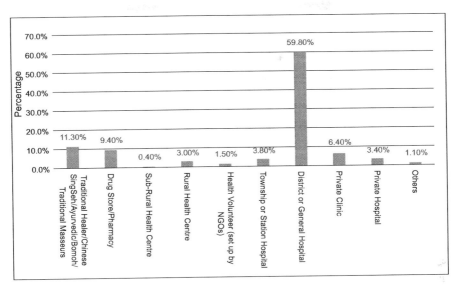

Figure 3.3 The most visited healthcare provider or facility
Source: Own calculations from the survey

or injury (they were asked to choose the top three answers). Figure 3.3 shows that the top most often visited facility is the district or general hospital, as 59.8 percent of them reported using it. Another 4 percent used the rural health centres (RHCs) and 0.4 percent visited sub-rural health centres (SRHCs). Of interest but not surprisingly, 11.3 percent sought treatment from traditional healers or alternative medical practitioners such as the Chinese *Sinseh*, or Indian *Ayurvedic* practitioner, *Bomoh* (shaman) or traditional *tukang urut* (masseurs). 9.4 percent used drugstores or the pharmacy, and 6.4 percent visited private clinics.

The level of satisfaction of respondents to the different healthcare facilities they used is shown in Figure 3.4. The figure shows high satisfaction levels for polyclinics and private doctors.

The responses on satisfaction of the various aspects of healthcare are shown in Figure 3.5.

On the experience of being treated respectfully, 54.2 percent reported that they were satisfied and 40.3 percent of them indicated "okay". Only 1.8 percent of the respondents were dissatisfied with their experiences of being treated respectfully while 3.7 percent of them did not have an opinion on this. About 49.6 percent of the respondents were satisfied with the way healthcare providers explained things to them and 38.3 percent of them were okay in this regard. Only 6.6 percent of the respondents reported that they were dissatisfied with how healthcare providers explained things to them and 5.5 percent of them

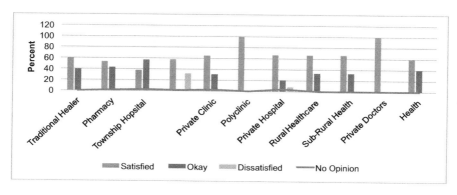

Figure 3.4 Satisfaction level with different available services
Source: Own calculations from the survey

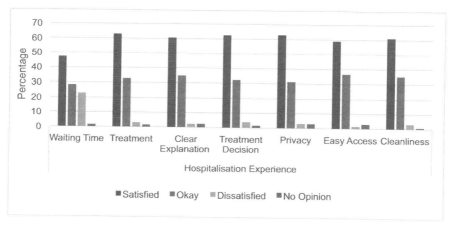

Figure 3.5 Level of older persons' satisfaction on various aspects of healthcare
Source: Own calculations from the survey

did not have an opinion on this. In contrast, nearly 50 percent of the respondents were satisfied with their experiences of being involved in making decisions on their treatment, while 39.4 of them were "okay" with their experiences. However, 10.2 percent of the respondents were dissatisfied with their experiences of being involved in making decisions for the treatment they received and 5.8 percent of them did not have an opinion on this.

Respondents were also asked about their level of satisfaction in relation to the way the health services ensured that they could talk privately to a healthcare provider. The figure showed that slightly more than half of the respondents (52.6 percent) reported to be "satisfied", and 37.6 percent of them thought that the healthcare services received were "okay". However, 2.2 percent of the respondents were dissatisfied with the way in which they could talk to the healthcare provider privately, while 7.7 percent of them did not have an opinion on this. Similarly, 51.5 percent of respondents reported being "satisfied" that they could see a healthcare provider and 42.3 percent of them were "okay" with regards to seeing a healthcare provider. However, there were 1.1 percent who were "dissatisfied", while 5.1 percent were non-committal on how they accessed a healthcare provider. In contrast, the qualitative data provided another view of the satisfaction levels of the OPs in this aspect. In one FGD with a group of rural Malay women, two women shared their negative experiences with health workers.

> If I was late or I did not see them on the date of the appointment, the worker would get mad at me. It caused 'headache' to me. But my children are working, so can't take day off on the previous appointment day. . . . The health personnel told me "Do you not love yourself anymore? You'll die if you continue doing this". I got headache after hearing all she said. It's not that we don't love ourselves . . . but she's being too straightforward . . . then she said. "You will not be able to walk anymore, you'll be disabled. Do you want that?
> (A rural woman, Malay, Sarawak)

Another woman said:

> They would easily get mad at us if we forget to take the medicine. "Why didn't you take your medicine?", she said. And I said, "I'm fasting so I can't take it". And then she answered, "Eat it then only you come back".
> (A rural woman, Malay, Sarawak)

In terms of respondents' satisfaction of the services, several disparaging comments were voiced:

1   "Some healthcare personnel tend to be rude".
2   "Doctors gave very little time to communicate and explained ailment".
3   "Some young doctors are not giving full attention, even distracted with their handphone".

In relation to cleanliness, 55.5 percent of the respondents were satisfied with the cleanliness of the health facility and 40.4 percent of them said "okay" on this point. However, 1.1 percent of the respondents were dissatisfied with the cleanliness of the health facility and 2.9 percent did not have an opinion on this.

In terms of satisfaction with the availability of medicine, the findings show that 60.1 percent of the respondents were satisfied with the availability of medicines, while 35.4 percent of them said 'okay' with the availability of medicines; 1.1 percent of the participants were dissatisfied with the availability of medicines and 3.3 percent of them did not have an opinion.

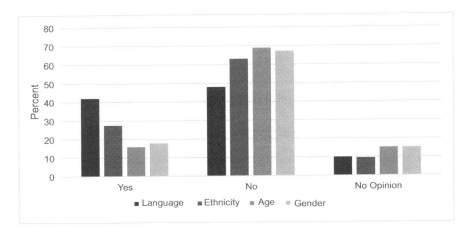

Figure 3.6 Preference in healthcare providers
Source: Own calculations from the survey

Respondents were asked if they have preference for healthcare providers in terms of language, ethnicity, gender and age. Generally, there were no strong preferences expressed by the respondents except for language, which was considered by many as important (Figure 3.6).

The results presented in Figure 3.6 show that 48 percent of the respondents did not have any preference for a doctor or healthcare provider in terms of language; in contrast, 42.1 percent of the respondents indicated a preference for a health provider in regard to the language of communication. On this matter, 9.9 percent of the respondents had no opinion. However, 63 percent of the respondents did not have any preference for a doctor or healthcare provider in terms of ethnic background, while 27.5 percent of them did have preference for a healthcare provider of a particular ethnic background. 9.5 percent of the respondents said they did not know. Similarly, 68.9 percent of the respondents did not have any preference for a doctor or healthcare provider in terms of age; in constrast, 15.9 percent of them did. 15.2 percent of the respondents did not have an opinion. In addition, more than 60 percent of the respondents showed no preference for a healthcare provider in terms of gender while 17.8 percent of them did. On this matter, 15.2 percent of the respondents were non-committal.

FGD with a group of urban women (ethnic Chinese) revealed that they preferred a female doctor for problems related to gynaecological issues. Furthermore, individual interviews with men of Indian background from Kuala Lumpur found that "there were issues of discrimination in serving the poorly educated senior citizens". Specifically, it was pointed out that "some healthcare personnel tend to raise their tone or were not so attentive to those who could not speak basic Malay or English, compared to those who can". The respondents who expressed preference in terms of the ethnicity of the doctors are related to the ease of communication because of language.

INPATIENT CARE

Figure 3.7 shows the respondents' satisfaction in terms of care and attention, medical treatment and availability of medicines.

Generally, respondents were satisfied with the care and attention, medical treatment and availability of medicine. As shown in the figure, 66.7 percent of the respondents were satisfied with the care and attention they received from the healthcare provider and 31.1 percent of them indicated "okay". However, 1.5 percent of the respondents were "dissatisfied" with the care and attention they received from the healthcare provider and 0.8 percent of them did not have an opinion. About 71.2 percent of the respondents were satisfied with the medical treatment they received and 27.3 percent of them were "okay" with it. However, 0.8 percent of the respondents were dissatisfied with the medical treatment received while another 0.8 percent did not have an opinion about it. The chart above shows that most of the respondents were satisfied with the availability of medicines (72.7 percent) and 25.8 percent of them were okay with it. However, 0.8 percent of the respondents were "dissatisfied" with the availability of medicine while another 0.8 percent did not have an opinion on this.

Figure 3.8 shows OPs' level of satisfaction on various aspects related to their hospitalisation experience. Most of the respondents were satisfied with the hospital experience expect when it came to waiting time. About 33 percent of the respondents said that they were "okay" with their experiences of being treated respectfully and 1.5 percent did not have an opinion on this.

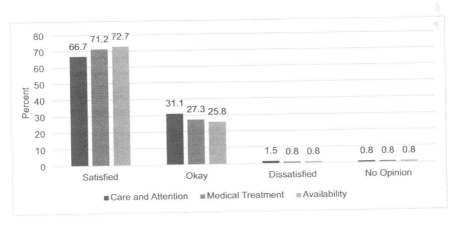

Figure 3.7 Satisfaction on respondents' on care and attention, medical treatment and availability of medicines

Source: Own calculations from the survey

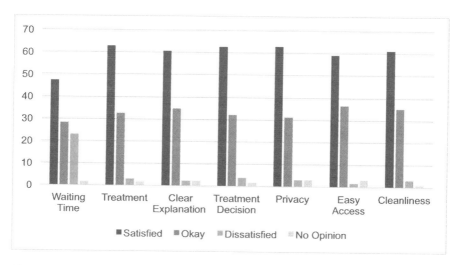

Figure 3.8 Hospitalisation experience
Source: Own calculations from the survey

On satisfaction with waiting time, 47.3 percent of respondents said that they were "satisfied" with the waiting time for their last hospital stay, and 22.9 percent of them said that they were "dissatisfied". On this point, 28.2 percent of respondents said that they were "okay" with the time waited for and 1.5 percent were non-committal.

The results show that 60.6 percent of the respondents were "satisfied" with the clear explanation of healthcare provider for their last hospital stay and 34.8 percent of them said "okay" on this matter. In contrast, 2.3 percent of the respondents reported "dissatisfied" and another 2.3 percent did not state an opinion. 62.6 percent of the respondents were "satisfied" with the experience of being involved in treatment decision for their last hospital stay and 32.1 percent of them were "okay" with it. However, 3.8 percent of the respondents were "dissatisfied" with the experience of being involved in treatment decision and 1.5 percent of them did not have an opinion.

On the question of whether respondents could talk privately to healthcare providers, 62.9 percent of the respondents said that they were "satisfied" while 31.1 percent of them said that they were "okay" with it. However, 3 percent of the respondents were "dissatisfied" with the way the health services ensured that they could talk privately to healthcare providers and 3 percent of them did not have an opinion on this. It was also found that 59.1 percent of the respondents were "satisfied" with the ease with which they could see a healthcare provider, but 1.5 percent of them reported being "dissatisfied". In contrast, 36.4 percent of the respondents said that they were "okay" with the ease with which they could see a healthcare provider

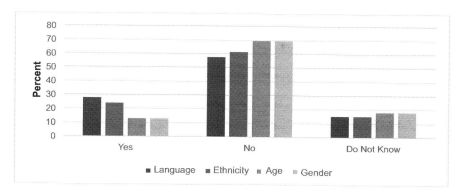

Figure 3.9 Preference of healthcare providers
Source: Own calculations from the survey

while 3 percent did not have an opinion on this. Moreover, 61.1 percent of the respondents said that they were "satisfied" with the cleanliness of the health facility during their last hospital stay; in contrast, 3.1 percent of them said that they were "dissatisfied" with it, while 35.1 percent indicated "okay" with the cleanliness of the health facility and 0.8 percent did not have an opinion.

In terms of preference for healthcare provider in the hospital setting, most respondents did not have specific preferences (Figure 3.9). The results show that 57.5 percent did not have any preference for a doctor or healthcare provider of a particular language, but 27.6 percent of them had a preference for a particular healthcare provider when it came to language. In contrast, 14.9 percent of the respondents did not have an opinion on this. Most of the respondents did not have a preference for a doctor or healthcare provider in terms of his or her ethnic background (61.2 percent), but 23.9 percent of them did have a preference for a healthcare provider of a particular ethnic group. In contrast, 14.9 percent of the respondents did not have an opinion. About 69.4 percent of the respondents did not have any preference for a doctor or healthcare provider in terms of age, but 12.7 percent of them did have a preference for a healthcare provider of a particular age. On this, 17.9 percent did not have an opinion. The finding showed that 69.4 percent of the respondents did not have any preference for a doctor or healthcare provider in terms of gender, but 12.7 percent of them did have a preference in this aspect. In this regard, 17.9 percent did not have an opinion on this.

Interestingly, the bio-data of the healthcare providers was not as important as when they sought outpatient treatment.

SALIENT ISSUES

1. Waiting time The dissatisfaction about waiting time applies to both inpatient and outpatient care and qualitative data show varying responses. From an FGD in Sarawak, rural women confirmed that they are aware about the priority given to OPs and appreciated that this has cut down on waiting time if they attended a clinic for common illnesses. However, if they need to go for a blood test and X-ray, they would need to go to another district and the waiting time would range from two to four hours. For those residing in the rural areas, a trip for a specialised check-up may mean that their family members, usually a son takes them in a vehicle and, in turn, would lose a day's work/pay. However, surprisingly, urban women reported in an FGD in Sarawak that they were not aware of priority given to OPs, nor were they aware that there was a priority lane for disabled persons and those who had been asked to fast the night before for a blood test. It was only during the FGDs that they realised there is a priority for OPs for seeing the doctor and receiving medication. One of them who attended a government specialist hospital on a periodical basis said this:

> I saw there is the label at the counter where we take our medicine which stated that it is for disabled persons and senior citizens. But no one queues there and there is no staff at that counter. Everyone queues up in the normal line. The queue is very long. Then I saw an old man walk to that counter and everything was done very fast. So I approached him and asked and he said that the counter was especially for senior citizens. However, no one told me that before. If you saw old people queuing there, you should actually tell them that they can use the fast lane for senior citizens. So after that I knew already. But at least the staff there should tell us. If they don't tell us, we have no idea.

In another FGD with mostly men, a very senior ex-government official gave a completely different view:

> And I am old, I am not working any more . . . I don't care about waiting time. Of course, if you go to the private clinic in 10 to 15 minutes you can be seen but in the government clinics maybe you have to wait for one hour or one and a half hours. But to me, that does not matter because I am old I have plenty of time. Maybe while waiting for the doctor I just leisurely watch people and happenings. Sometimes you meet a friend, then you can chit chat, and sometimes you make new friends in the clinic.

He went on to suggest that the waiting areas could be improved by having more comfortable chairs and better air conditioning and an atmosphere to make the wait time pleasant.

In another FGD with ex-medical officials, a former nursing practitioner explained that measures to reduce the waiting period for some specialist treatments have been introduced by providing a service for full-payment patients who can have their operation expedited outside the usual office hours. One example is the heart specialist centre. As added by another senior medical official,

"This was done not only to benefit the patients, but also to allow the doctors in public hospitals to earn extra income in addition to their salary". This no doubt facilitates the reduction of the waiting period and expedites treatment for those in need of specialist services; however, such an arrangement leaves OPs with low income, particularly those from rural regions, without the needed services.

2. *Autonomy and decision-making by older persons themselves* On the question of autonomy of the OPs to be able to make decisions about seeking treatment and hospitalisation, the answers revealed a heavy family involvement. The findings showed that for treatment, 61.6 percent of the respondents made decisions for themselves, followed by 23.2 percent who had their son or daughter make decisions for them; 14 percent had their spouse or partner, 0.7 percent had non-family members and 0.4 percent had other family members decide on the treatment on behalf of the OP. Decisions on hospitalisation showed even less autonomy held in the hands of OPs. Nearly half (48.2 percent) of the respondents made their own decisions about their hospitalisation, while decisions made by others are as follows: their son or daughter (27.7 percent), their spouse and partner (22.3 percent), other family members (0.9 percent) and non-family members (0.9 percent).

FGDs with rural women highlighted the extent of family in decision-making pertaining to treatment and healthcare. All doctor's appointments are subjected to their children and family members' discretion. Children and kin played significant roles in supporting OPs in terms of providing care for their health and to ensure that they keep their doctor's appointments and medical check-ups. They would follow their children's advice and all appointments and visits to the health centre are managed by their children and kin. Among them, staying healthy is very important so that they would not be a burden to their children and other family members.

3. *Information accessibility* Women and indigenous minority members have less access to information. For example, an *Orang Asli* man was asked about his knowledge of health policies, and in his reply he said:

> Don't know, never heard of. In the past when young always went out of the village, don't have TV at home. Now have TV and electricity, but also don't know.

A comparison made between knowledge and awareness of health schemes and priorities between men and women highlighted unequal accessibility between the two. Figure 3.10 shows that 13.4 percent of the male respondents were aware of current healthcare schemes targeting OPs, while 11 percent of women were also aware of the same schemes; in contrast, 34.8 percent of male respondents were not aware of current healthcare schemes for OPs, whereas 40.1 percent of female respondents were not aware of these schemes.

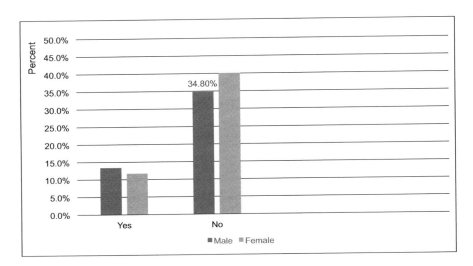

Figure 3.10 Awareness of the current healthcare scheme targeting older people
Source: Own calculations from the survey

Although in every division in each state of Malaysia, there is at least one health education unit which conducts awareness raising campaigns such as road shows to disseminate information, however, when reaching out to OPs, this remains a challenge.

4. Perception of health rights Answers to the question pertaining to OPs' perception of healthcare as a right clearly showed that the idea of rights have not taken root among the respondents of the study. Common answers are as follows.

> Can't ask for more as a man who has little education.
>
> (IDI, Indian man, 61 years old, Selangor)

> I don't expect the government to give me my rights, it is more a matter of we OPs having to take care of our own health.
>
> (FGD, Urban women, Chinese)

The idea of rights seemed to be understood more from the perspective of what (more) could the government provide for OPs. The response from a Chinese woman living in an urban area is indicative of this line of thought:

> More can be done in terms of basic facilities to promote healthy ageing; for example, in Singapore there is a small park in every residential area for older people to exercise.

3.5   Discussion, policy implications and conclusions

In Malaysia, healthcare is premised on the model of universal health coverage through the provision of a long established public healthcare system and the recent expansion of private health services. For OPs, various policies and guidelines have been developed with the objectives of providing age friendly, affordable, accessible and culturally acceptable healthcare services. The findings of the study suggest that there remain gaps and challenges to meet the objective of health security for all older Malaysians in various parts of the country.

First, on availability and accessibility of healthcare, outpatient facilities are reported to be available since they are mostly located in the village or town of OPs. However, for some groups of OPs, the condition of the road and the means of transport to get to these health facilities present barriers in accessing healthcare. The inadequacy of a good public transport system and the physical condition of the OPs necessitate the assistance and support of family to access health services. This is more so for inpatient care, as hospitals are located in major cities and towns. For rural OPs who more often than not are also from low-income communities, accessing inpatient care may be a complex process in which many may not have the autonomy to make decisions for themselves. Accessing healthcare is not only based on their personal decision but also carers, especially their children who may be taking on the financial responsibilities including paying for the treatment, visitation and spending time to assist OPs in accessing health facilities.

Second, closely tied to accessibility is affordability. While health service and medicines for common diseases is almost free (with one Malaysian ringgit as registration fee, and free for OPs), indirect and opportunity costs, such as the cost of transport to and from health facilities and their homes and of taking time away from work among the carers, may well deter OPs from accessing healthcare, particularly in terms of inpatient care and specialist services.

Third, in terms of acceptability, many important issues come to the fore in this study. The socioeconomic status, demographic background and educational level of OPs and their carers are seen to influence choices in selecting healthcare providers and even whether or not to seek treatment or hospital admission (Selvaratnam, Bakar and Haji Idris 2012; Yong 2015). Furthermore, acceptability of healthcare services has proven to either attract or distract decisions to access healthcare services (Yamada, Chen, Naddeo and Harris 2015). While acceptability of the 'modern' healthcare system is gaining ground among OPs in rural communities, traditional healers continue to be sought after. Whether this is entirely a result of the dominance of traditional beliefs among OPs or the fact that traditional healers provide them with a much more accessible, affordable and culturally relevant alternative to 'modern' healthcare is an area worthy of further research.

This leads to the next point, which relates to the training of health personnel at all levels of healthcare providers. Not only should health officials be equipped with knowledge on geriatric medicine, but also skills on interpersonal relationship building with OPs. In designing and constructing healthcare provisions and service delivery for OPs, it is important to acknowledge differences in the experiences of OPs in terms of gender, education level, socioeconomic and class status and geographical locations.

The experiences of the OPs in the study highlighted the glaring disparity between urban and rural regions not only in terms of availability and accessibility of healthcare facilities, but also in terms of the quality of services and the way health personnel relate to them. This inequity in the distribution and utilisation of healthcare services put OPs in the rural regions from lower income and indigenous minorities at a disadvantage, denying them of the health security entitled to them. If the government is serious about achieving the objectives of the National Health Policy of the Older Persons 2008, addressing the inequity and ensuring that quality, standard healthcare enjoyed by all older Malaysians is definitely the way forward.

Some important questions have been raised in the foregoing discussions in relation to the provision of healthcare for OPs in Malaysia. What direction are we heading to in healthcare policies for OPs? What do health security and rights mean for the OPs in Malaysia? While the authors do not claim to provide answers to these questions, it would appear that recognising the trend of a growing ageing population and acknowledging the place of OPs in our society entails policies and programmes emanating from a rights perspective.

Note

1 Previously, the people in the community took almost two days to access the nearest town by foot. Because of the current improvement in roads and land transportation, they are now able to cut short the travel time to half a day to get to the nearest town to access healthcare services.

References

Chee, Heng Leng and Simon Barraclough (eds.) (2009) *Health Care in Malaysia: The Dynamics of Provision, Financing and Access.* Oxon and New York: Routledge.

Chen, C.Y.P., Andrews, G.R., Josef, R., Chan, K.E. and J.T. Arokiasamy (1986) *Health and Ageing in Malaysia, Kuala Lumpur: Faculty of Medicine.* University of Malaya.

Country Report (2013) "Country Report Malaysia". URL: <www.mhlw.go.jp/bunya/kokusaigyomu/asean/2013/dl/Malaysia_CountryReport.pdf> (accessed 20 July 2017).

Department of Statistics (2017) URL: <www.dosm.gov.my> (accessed 10 June 2017).

Dillip, Angel, Alba, Sandra, Mshana, Christopher, Hetzel, Manuel W., Lengeler, Christian, Mayumana, Iddy and Brigit Obrist (2012) "Acceptability – A Neglected Dimension of Access to Health Care: Findings From a Study on Childhood Convulsions in Rural Tanzania". *BMC Health Services Research*, 12: 113. URL: <http://doi.org/10.1186/1472-6963-12-113.>

Evans, David B., Hsu, Justine and Ties Boerma (2013) "Universal Health Coverage and Universal Access". *Bulletin of the World Health Organization*, 91: 546–546A. URL: <http://dx.doi.org/10.2471/BLT.13.125450>

Human Rights Commission of Malaysia (2015) *Report on Care Services for Older Persons and Support for Caregivers.* Kuala Lumpur: Human Rights Commission of Malaysia.

Lim, Teck Onn, Sivasampu, Sheamini, AriZa, Z. and M.K. Nabilah (2011) "Overview on hospitals and specialists services in Malaysia", In *National Healthcare Establishments & Workforce Statistics 2008–2009,* edited by Sheamini Sivasampu, Lim Teck Onn and Noor Hishan Abdullah. Kuala Lumpur: Ministry of Health. URL: <http://www.crc.gov.my/nhsi/wp-content/uploads/publications/NHEWS_PrimaryCare/chapter1.pdf> (accessed 25 July 2017).

Ministry of Health (2002) *Guidelines on Oral Healthcare for the Elderly in Malaysia.* Putrajaya: Oral Health Division Ministry of Health Malaysia. URL: <https://www.mah.se/upload/FAKULTETER/OD/Avdelningar/who/WPRO/Malaysia/data/oral_healthcare_for_the_elderly_in_malaysia.pdf> (accessed 25 July 2017).

———— (2009) *Clinical Practice Guidelines on Management of Dementia* (2nd ed.). Putrajaya: Ministry of Health Malaysia. URL: <http://www.moh.gov.my/penerbitan/CPG2017/4484.pdf> (accessed 25 July 2017).

Ministry of Health, Annual Report (2014) Putra Jaya: Ministry of Health Malaysia. URL: <http://www.moh.gov.my/images/gallery/publications/Annual%20Report%202014.pdf> (accessed 20 July 2017).

National Health Policy for Older Persons (2008) Kuala Lumpur: Ministry of Health Malaysia URL: <http://fh.moh.gov.my/v3/index.php/component/jdownloads/send/23-sektor-kesihatan-warga-emas/260-dasarkesihatanwargaemas?option=com_jdownloads> (accessed 25 July 2017).

Ng, Sor Tho, Tengku-Aizan, Hamid and Nai Peng Tey (2011) "Perceived Health Status and Daily Activity Participation of Older Malaysians". *Asia Pacific Journal of Public Health,* 23(4): 470–84.

Ong Fong Sim and Wong Lee Leong (2002) "Living Arrangement and Long-term Care of Elderly in Malaysia". Unpublished Research Report, Faculty of Business and Accountancy, University of Malaya, Kuala Lumpur, cited in Ong Fong Sim (2009) "Health Care and Long-term Care Issues for the Elderly". In *Health Care in Malaysia: The Dynamics of Provision, Financing and Access,* edited by Chee Heng Leng and S. Barraclough. Oxon and New York: Routledge.

Selvaratnam, D.P., Bakar, Norliala Abu and Nor Aini Haji Idris (2012) "The Health Determinant of Elderly Malaysian Population". Proceeding PERKEM VII, Jilid 2, pp. 1195–99.

Sherina Mohd Sidik, Lekhraj Rampal and Mustaqim Afifi (2004, January) "Physical and Mental Health Problems of the Elderly in a Rural Community of Sepang". *Selangor Malaysian Journal of Medical Sciences,* 11(1): 52–9.

Siti Zaharah Jamaluddin, Jal Zabdi Mohd Yusoff Usharani Balasingam, Zulazhar Tehir, Sridevi Thambapillay, and Mohammad Abu Taher (eds.) (2017) *Protecting the Elderly Against Abuse and Neglect: Legal and Social Strategies.* Kuala Lumpur: University of Malaya Press.

Siop, Sidiah (2003) *Health Needs of Older People in a Semi-urban Village in Malaysia.* Kota Samarahan: Universiti Malaysia Sarawak.

———— (2008) "Disability and Quality of Life of Non-Institutionalized Older Malaysian". Unpublished PhD Thesis, Universiti Putra Malaysia.

Siop, Sidiah., Verbrugge, L.M. and Hamid Tengku Aizan (2008) "Disability and Quality of Life Among Older Malaysians". URL: <paa2008.princeton.edu/papers/80962>

Tengku Aizan, Hamid (2015) *Population Ageing: A Mosaic of Issues, Challenges and Prospects*. Serdang: Universiti Putra Malaysia Press.

Tengku Aizan, Hamid and Yahaya Nurizan (2008) "National Policy for the Elderly in Malaysia: Achievements and Challenges". In *Ageing in Southeast and East Asia: Family, Social Protection and Policy Challenges*, edited by Lee Hock Guan. Singapore: Institute of Southeast Asian Studies.

United Nations Department of Economic and Social Affairs (UNDESA) (2015) *The Population Prospects: 2015 Revision*. New York: UNDESA.

Wan-Ibrahim, W.A. and I. Zainab (2014) "Health Conditions of Older Persons in Rural Malaysia". *World Applied Sciences Journal*, 30(7): 903–6.

Yamada, Tetsuji, Chen, Chia-Chin., Naddeo, J.J. and Joseph R. Harris (2015) "Changing Healthcare Policies: Implications for Income, Education, and Health Disparity". *Frontiers in Public Health*, 3: 195. URL: <https://doi.org/10.3389/fpubh.2015.00195>

Yong, Kang Cheah (2015) "Socioeconomic Determinants of Health Enhancing Expenditure Among the Elderly in Malaysia: An Ethnic Comparison". *Journal Ekonomi Malaysia*, 49(1): 93–102.

Zaiton, A., Nor Afiah, Mohd Zulkefli and Abdul LatiffLatiffah (2006) "Functional Status of the Elderly Residing in Public Funded Shelter Homes in Peninsular Malaysia". *Asia-Pacific Journal of Public Health*, 18(Supplement): 60–3.

4 Thailand

Chalermpol Chamchan, Rossarin Gray
and Kusol Soonthorndhada

4.1 Introduction

The number of older persons (OPs) in Thailand has grown rapidly and will continue to do so in future decades. Since 1960, the number of OPs aged 60 and over in the Thai population has increased seven-fold from approximately 1.5 million to 11.3 million in 2017, or 17 percent of the total population. The latest population projections for Thailand illustrate just how extensive the future growth of both the number of OPs and their share of the population are likely to be in the next three and a half decades. Future population ageing will occur even more rapidly, with the proportion of OPs projected to increase to 20 percent by 2021 and 28 percent by 2031, at which point Thailand will be considered a "Complete Aged Society" and a "Super Aged Society", respectively.

As in other countries in the world, population ageing in Thailand is a result of an increase in life expectancy and decrease in fertility rates of the population. Vapattanawong and Prasartkul (2014) and the Institute for Population and Social Research (2017) have documented that the increasing share of OPs is largely driven by the reduction of total fertility rate from around 6.0 live births per woman in 1965–1970 to around 1.7 in 2005–2006 and 1.59 in 2017. The number of births declined significantly from more than 1 million during 1963–1983 to 0.74 million in 2015. In contrast, life expectancy at birth continually increased from 61 years to around 75 years in 1976 to 2015, respectively.

This chapter aims to undertake an analysis of the findings from a qualitative research study conducted on the health security situation of OPs in the context of Thailand. The discussion provides an overview of population ageing in Thailand, the health status of OPs and their access to health protection coverage and existing health schemes, provisions of healthcare services for OPs and OPs' opinions of accessibility, acceptability and affordability to appropriate healthcare.

4.2 Health status of Thai older persons

Health is a key concern for an aged society including Thailand. Increasing life expectancy has led to higher expectations not only to live longer, but to live longer with lower levels of morbidity and fewer years of disability, and with a high quality of life. In the case of Thailand, although the results from various sources are somewhat mixed, they point more to an improvement in overall health of OPs than a deterioration. The top three problems about older adults' physical health are movement, hearing and vision (Foundation of Thai Gerontology Research and Development Institute 2017), according to the most recent National Health Examination Survey in 2014; the percentages of those with impaired walking, hearing problems and impaired near vision (with/without glasses) were found to be lower as compared to the results from the previous survey in 2009. These percentages were 15.7 percent, 24.5 percent and 44.0 percent, respectively, in 2014 (Aekplakorn 2014), declining from 18.6 percent, 28.0 percent and 46.5 percent, respectively, in 2009 (Aekplakorn 2009). The prevalence of dementia as screened by the Thai Mini-Mental State Examination was also found to have decreased from 12.4 percent in 2009 to 8.1 percent in 2014. Among the OPs aged 80 years whose dementia prevalence was the highest compared to other age groups, the percentage of prevalence had also decreased from 32.5 percent to 22.6 percent (Aekplakorn 2014). Assessed by their self-rated health, the results show that, although the percentage of OPs that assessed their health during the past week as "good" or "very good" fluctuated between 2011 and 2014, the percentages that said their health was either "poor" or "very poor" were lower in both 2011 (15.9 percent) and 2014 (16.0 percent) than in 2007 (24.3 percent) (National Statistical Office 2014).

The most updated health profiles of OPs can be drawn out from the results of the National Health and Welfare Survey in 2015 (National Statistical Office 2015). When asked to compare current health status with their health status in the past year, the majority of OPs (51.3 percent) reported that it was the "same". Slightly more than one-third (35.2 percent) perceived worse health, and only 7.8 percent perceived better health. On the perception of general health conditions at the day of interview, 55.8 percent reported "moderate" level, 23.2 percent reported "good" and 17.4 percent reported "bad". Regarding health problems difficulties, 62 percent reported to have no physical constraints, 85.5 percent and 76.0 percent had no difficulties with self-care activities and activities of daily living (ADLs), respectively and 72.6 percent reported that they had no mental health problems.

On minor illnesses in the past one month (outpatient illnesses that did not need admission in a healthcare facility), 46.2 percent of OPs reported a kind of sickness, of which 17.9 percent recorded general diseases or illness symptoms and 27.3 percent recorded chronic diseases. The outpatient sickness rate (both those as a result of general illnesses and chronic diseases) appeared to increase with age of OPs. Chronic diseases were the cause of outpatient sickness of OPs more in urban areas than those in rural areas, the richer (by income quintiles) than the poorer ones. In the past 12 months, 6.9 percent of OPs had never been admitted in a health facility (inpatient sickness). The inpatient admission rate was higher in rural areas than in urban areas (7.3 percent and 6.5 percent) and, similarly to outpatient illnesses, this seemed to increase with the age of OPs. The rate among OPs aged 60–69 years was 5.8 percent while those aged

70–79 and 80 years old and over were 7.6 percent and 10.3 percent, respectively. By income quintiles, the rate was found higher among poorer OPs and was highest among those in the poorest quintile.

Overall, more than half (55.7 percent) of OPs reported having at least one chronic disease, of which 41.1 percent had hypertension, 26.1 percent had diabetes, 4.5 percent had osteoarthritis, 3.7 percent had heart disease and 3.1 percent had high cholesterol. The percentage of OPs with co-morbidity of two, three and four chronic diseases were 22.4 percent, 6.8 percent and 1.5 percent, respectively. By characteristics of OPs, females (60.5 percent) had higher prevalence rates of chronic diseases than males (49.9 percent). The prevalence was higher for persons living in urban areas (59.3 percent) compared with those from the rural ones (53.3 percent), and it increased with age of the persons (48.8 percent, 64.0 percent and 66.5 percent of those aged 60–69, 70–79 and 80 years old and over, respectively). Chronic morbidity also appeared to be more prevalent among OPs with higher incomes.

4.3 Health systems and policies focusing on older persons

All Thai older people have access to free government health services under the "Universal Health Coverage" scheme (UHCS). Universal minimal cost or free health coverage at government facilities has been available since 2002 for all nationals regardless of age. However, persons aged 60 and over have been entitled to free government medical services including exemption even from the minimal fee since 1992. OPs also benefit as retired workers or parents and spouses of workers who have been employed in the public sector since they are entitled to such benefits under the Civil Servant Medical Benefit Scheme (CSMBS) compared to those under the UHCS plan.

According to the 2015 National Health and Welfare Survey, it can be said that all Thai OPs are universally entitled to and protected from catastrophic health expenditure by at least a public health scheme in terms of health scheme coverage. The majority of them (about four-fifths or 80.1 percent) were covered by the UHCS and 15.8 percent were covered by the CSMBS. A small percentage (1.8 percent) was registered with and covered by the Social Security Scheme (SSS), which is the health scheme that provides health financial protection to workers currently employed in the private sector. The health benefit package offered by the SSS is similar to the UHCS although with slight differences. Apart from health benefits, the SSS also provides other social security benefits to its beneficiaries including old-age benefits, and financial compensation in the case of death and disabilities from work. After retiring from work in the private sector, OPs under the SSS can choose to be covered under the UHCS. Results from the 2015 Survey revealed that less than 1 percent of the OPs in Thailand were left unprotected by any heath scheme. By area of living and income quintiles, the UHCS' coverage appeared larger among OPs living in rural areas and those in poor income quintiles, while those covered under CSMBS and SSS were mostly living in the urban areas and from the higher income quintiles. The coverage distribution seemed not much different by gender and age group.

4.4   Assessing health security among older persons in Thailand

4.4.1   Assessment methods

Both quantitative and qualitative methods of data collection are used in this study. Quantitative findings illustrating demographic and health profiles of Thai OPs, their health security coverage, care-seeking behaviour and service health utilisation were mainly compiled and analysed from the secondary datasets of the 2014 Survey of Older Persons in Thailand and the 2015 Survey on Health and Welfare, both of which were national representative surveys conducted by the National Statistical Office (NSO) of Thailand.

A qualitative research fieldwork exercise – as a case study – was conducted in Sankamphaeng District of Chiangmai province in northern Thailand, with specific aims to investigate in-depth situations of health and access to appropriate healthcare among OPs, health service delivery and health systems for OPs at the community level, unmet needs and vulnerable groups of OPs who should be targeted for support and other related issues. The district was purposively selected according to the fine reputation of its District Health System (DHS) operations and the possibility of the research team in accessing OPs and key respondents from public health facilities including Sub-district Health Promotion Hospitals (SHPH) and community hospitals, local government organisations and other local government bodies and stakeholders for interviews. The fieldwork was undertaken in January 2017. Data collection was conducted both in urban and rural settings. Focused-group discussions (FGDs) with OPs were conducted in both urban and rural settings. In total, ten in-depth interviews and four FGDs were conducted.

The focus of the chapter will be on findings from the fieldwork relating to the provision of healthcare services by public healthcare providers mainly at health facilities under the Ministry of Public Health (MOPH) of Thailand with cooperation or support from the local government and involving stakeholders (Figure 4.1). Under the MOPH, healthcare services will be provided in response to the health needs of each group of OPs characterised by stages of health condition. In regard to this, OPs in each community are screened by their health condition and grouped into three categories: (a) the "society-ridden", who are mostly independent and who do not need assistance or care from others, and enjoy socialising or contact with others in the community; (b) the "home-ridden", who are self-dependent (might be with a minor disability, some chronic diseases or psychological disorder) and are able to take care of themselves and do not need much assistance or care from others. The latter group are less likely to socialise with others in the community or may prefer to stay at home and not go out to

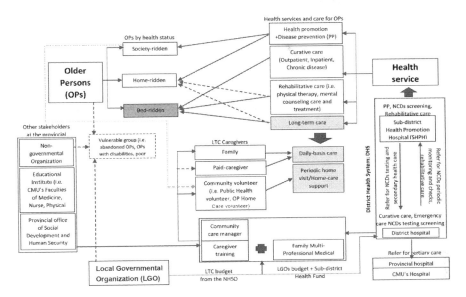

Figure 4.1 Health service and care for OPs – qualitative case study in Chiangmai province

Source: Own illustrations

participate in social activities. This group is considered "physically healthy" but a group with high risk for "psychological problems" and other possible health problems in the future. It is among this group that older people require more social participation; and, (c) the "bed-ridden", who include persons with disabilities and who need comprehensive assistance and long-term care from others for nearly all their ADLs.

A health screening template of "geriatric syndrome" is used as a tool to assess health conditions and screen possible health risks of OPs (i.e. in terms of ADLs dependency, diabetes mellitus (DM), hypertension and psychological problems). The score from the screening result is used as a criterion for grouping OPs in one of the following categories: "society ridden", "home-ridden" and "bed-ridden". From the fieldwork in Chiangmai province, on average, the distribution of OPs by these categories in the visited communities are about 80–90 percent for the society-ridden, about 5–15 percent for the home-ridden and about 5 percent or less for the bed-ridden. It was observed that the percentage of home-ridden is higher in the urban settings than in the rural settings. OPs in the rural areas were found to participate more in social-cultural activities in the community, which reflects their stronger social capital compared with OPs living in the urban areas.

Basically, provision of care and service by public hospitals either at the provincial or district levels and the SHPH at the sub-district level include health promotion and disease prevention (or "PP"), curative care and rehabilitative care. In particular for the older population group, long-term care needs to be addressed. However, the provision and delivery of long-term care – and also healthcare services – in many cases, is not responsible solely by the public health sector but with support and cooperation from other stakeholders including local government organisations and other governmental agencies.

The PP services for OPs include periodic OP's health screening and monitoring (especially for persons with chronic diseases), provision of health knowledge and education (in particular, healthy food consumption and tips for exercising), support for health promotion activities in the community such as regular group exercises (aerobics and stick play) or meditation classes. The PP services are mainly delivered by primary healthcare facilities at the sub-district level or the SHPH. Curative care includes care for outpatient and inpatient illnesses, chronic diseases, emergency care, dental care and psychological care. Primary curative care can be delivered at the SHPH in the sub-district level and in the case of the most severe conditions, under the referral system of the Thai public health system, older patients will be transferred to the community hospital (at district level) for secondary care and to the general hospital (at provincial level) or the regional hospital for tertiary care, respectively. Rehabilitative care for OPs is mainly for those with minor strokes or those needing physical therapy (for example, OPs with osteoarthritis, who have experienced falls or who have undergone surgeries). The provision of rehabilitation found in Chiangmai is mostly delivered at the SHPH and, in some cases, a rehabilitation centre is established in the community with support from the local government, community leaders and volunteers.

The provision and delivery of care will be targeted differently by public health providers for OPs according to their health condition and needs. Health promotion and disease prevention services are targeted at the society-ridden facilitation and support for participation in social activities including volunteer efforts to promote good health physically, mentally and socially. The home-ridden are also targeted for health promotion and disease prevention services together with encouragement to have more social participation and interaction with others in the community. Curative and rehabilitative care might also be needed depending on the illnesses and health difficulties of each person. The bed-ridden are the group that need long-term care (LTC), including both direct care and indirect care. Direct care includes care and support to the OPs for daily activities which is mainly provided by the primary caregiver and family members, and healthcare, mainly curative and rehabilitative care, which is delivered by the Family Multi-Professional Medical Team (from the hospital or the SHPH) with support from the local government. Indirect care and support include periodic home visits and the provision of caregiver training and moral support. These can be provided by public health staff from the SHPH or Community Public Health Volunteers, Community Older Persons Home Care Volunteers and other groups comprising community members, providing moral support in term of visits or material support from the local government.

In terms of LTC for older persons, although caregiving on a daily basis is still mainly undertaken by the OP's family members or relatives, the Thai government is aware of the challenges that LTC poses in the context of decreasing availability of family assistance. Extending the 2008–2011 Plan, the Health Development Strategic Plan for the Elderly (2013–2023) of the MoPH spells out a strategy for dealing with this. It is based on the concept that the quality of life of OPs in the older age cohorts can be best retained through a combination of assistance within their family and a supporting system provided by healthcare and social services within their own community. The plan emphasises the need for the community and local administrative organisations to cooperate in implementing this plan, including allocating a budget for the purpose. The components of the system include databases on OPs, good-quality elderly clubs, community volunteers and the Family Multi-Professional Medical Team to provide home-based care for OPs, preventive dental services and a system to ensure care for persons who are home- or bed-bound (Foundation of Thai Gerontology Research and Development Institute 2012).

The Bureau of Empowerment for Older Persons (now Department of Older Persons) launched the Home Care Volunteers for the Elderly Program in 2003. Its objective is to establish a system of community-based care and protection for OPs with chronic illnesses, especially for those who are bed-ridden and have no caregivers or who are underprivileged. This volunteer programme employs the concept of self-help groups or peer support in its implementation. In many cases, the home care volunteers are the OPs in the same community who are in the society-ridden group. The volunteer works for the home-ridden and bed-ridden and provides benefits not only to receivers of care but also to the givers or the society-ridden in terms of the feeling of pride and self-value in helping others, improved mental health, having social participation, and prolonging of the healthy stage of life. This is consistent with the "Active Ageing" concept and also benefits the main caretaker of the home-ridden and bed-ridden OPs in terms of having more social interaction with others, improved mental health, moral support and other forms of support. After its initial start as a pilot programme, it steadily expanded and attained some level of coverage in all communities throughout Thailand in 2013. However, the extent and quality of services provided by OP home care volunteers vary greatly across communities. For instance, only one-third of local authorities surveyed in a recent evaluation study reported that services provided by OP home care volunteers met the needs of elders in their communities (Suwanrada 2014). Long-term institutional residences for the aged are considered only as a last resort to be provided by the Thai government as a way of dealing with persons in need of eldercare. Thus, there are only 12 institutional old-age homes supported by the national government with under 2000 residents, and 13 others under the supervision of the Department of Local Administration (Foundation of Thai Gerontology Research and Development Institute 2012).

4.4.2   Key findings

Accessibility

As mentioned earlier, the universal healthcare coverage policy of the Thai government since 2002 guarantees the "rights" of access to timely and appropriate healthcare services to all Thai citizens, including OPs with a protection of catastrophic financial expenditure through three existing health schemes: the UHCS, the CSMBS and the SSS.

HEALTH PROMOTION AND DISEASE PREVENTION

The 2014 Survey of the Older Persons in Thailand included questions on whether the respondent had gone for a physical check-up unrelated to a specific illness during the past 12 months and about receiving of home visits by health staff and home care volunteers. The results showed that in total just over half of Thais 60 or older (52 percent) reported that they had a check-up in the previous year (of which 49 percent at a public health facility and 3 percent at a private one). The percentage is modestly lower than indicated in the 2011 Survey of Older Persons (56 percent), based on an identical question and varies very little by age, gender or area of residence of the OPs.

Physical check-ups are one of the health services that are provided free under government healthcare coverage. Still the overwhelming predominance of the government health service as the main healthcare provider is not surprising. Such check-ups are typically heavily subsidised and likely to be less expensive when provided by the government compared to private sources and are also more convenient to access as well as provided at no cost. Apart from medical check-ups, slightly over half (52 percent) of the OPs indicated that they had received a home visit either from health personnel or from the Community Home Care Volunteers. The prevalence of visits from each source increases with the age of the respondent. There is a slight difference, however, with respect to gender, but home visits of both types are distinctively more common for rural than urban elderly. Receiving community assistance is also quite a common service and likely reflects the increased emphasis on community-based approaches to assist the elderly population.

OUTPATIENT CARE

On outpatient care-seeking behaviour (of the last illness in the past month), according to the results of the 2015 Survey on Health and Welfare, among OPs who fell sick, the majority (24 percent) visited a general hospital for care, 20.7 percent visited the SHPH, 19.5 percent visited a community hospital, 11 percent bought medicine from a drugstore and 4 percent reported to have received no treatment.

Among those who received outpatient treatment, 60.9 percent utilised health benefits under the UHCS, 14.3 percent under the CSMBS, around 1 percent under the SSS, while about one-fifth (21.4 percent) did not utilise benefits from any health scheme and instead relied on out-of-pocket (OOP) payment. The key reasons among those who did not utilise any of the benefits from the health schemes they were entitled to were minor sickness (53 percent), long waiting time and long queues (21.5 percent), doubt about quality of drug prescribed (6.4 percent), operating time constraint (6.4 percent) and that the health facility was located far away from the residence of the person (3.9 percent).

The outpatient care-seeking behaviour appeared different by characteristics of the OPs. For those in rural areas, the majority reported to visit SHPH for care, followed by the community hospital, general hospital and drugstore. For those residing in "urban areas", the largest percentage visited the general hospital followed by the non-MOPH public hospital and community hospital. By income quintiles, the richest quintile (Q5) – compared to other quintiles – visited the general hospitals, non-MOPH hospitals and private hospitals for care. The poorer quintiles visited the SHPH and community hospitals much more for care. By health schemes, the UHCS beneficiaries more than the beneficiaries of other schemes tended to utilise the SHPH and community hospitals, while those who accessed the SSS were more likely to utilise the care provided at private hospitals and general hospitals. The CSMBS' beneficiaries utilised care mostly at general hospitals and non-MOPH hospitals.

INPATIENT CARE

On inpatient care-seeking behaviour (of the last admission in the past year according to the 2015 Survey), among those who fell ill, the majority (48.5 percent) was admitted at a general hospital, 32.7 percent was at a community hospital, 9.8 percent was at a private hospital and 6.2 percent at a non-MOPH public hospital. On reasons for choosing the hospital for the last inpatient admission, the majority at 52.8 percent reported that decisions were circumscribed by the health scheme to which the person was entitled, 12.5 percent was assigned by the referral system and 11.9 percent saw the healthcare provider depending on the availability of the specialist physician. On the question of who is the main caregiver after one's discharge from the hospital, about 17.6 percent of OPs reported having no caretaker, 37.2 percent received care from a son or daughter and 32.8 percent received care from a spouse.

Among those who received inpatient treatment, 71.2 percent utilised the health benefits provided by the UHCS, 14.7 percent by the CSMBS and 1.2 percent by the SSS. The percentage of those who did not utilise benefits from any health scheme was 7.0 percent. Key reasons for not utilising the benefits were linked to long waiting times and queues, no available specialist physician in the hospital designated by the health scheme one was entitled to, constraint of operating time of contracted health facility, the distance of the location of contracted health facility from where the patient resides, needed inpatient treatment was not covered by the health scheme and doubt on quality of drug prescribed.

On inpatient care utilisation, the pattern of admission at general hospitals and community hospitals was found to be fairly similar between OPs residing in rural areas and those in urban areas. However, the admission at private hospitals and non-MOPH hospitals was apparently higher among urban elders. By income quintiles, the richest quintile (Q5) compared to other quintiles was admitted for inpatient treatment more than at a private hospital, while less so at a general hospital and community hospital. In contrast, the poorer quintiles were admitted more at a general hospital and a community hospital. By health scheme, the UHCS' beneficiaries were admitted at a community hospital and general hospital, while the SSS beneficiaries were admitted at private hospitals, non-MOPH public hospitals and university hospitals. In contrast, the CSMBS beneficiaries were admitted at general hospitals and non-MOPH public hospitals.

ACCESSIBILITY IN THE URBAN AND RURAL AREA SETTINGS

Interviews from the fieldwork conducted in the Chiangmai province found that access to a higher level of care and service at public hospitals (community and general hospitals) appeared to be more convenient (i.e. closer distance and less transportation expenses) in the urban areas compared to OPs living in rural areas. However, the strength of social support and networks in urban areas are much weaker than in rural areas. Community members are more independent, making self-help or peer support, or social activities, more limited (as compared to those in rural areas).

The emerging challenge shows up in the private clustered habitat or privately-run villages, which are increasing in terms of numbers and areas in many urban settings. Such clustered areas are privately-owned, which is difficult for public health staff to work in because of a myriad of reasons: lack of information about village members in terms of numbers and demographic profiles; some members, especially OPs, are a hidden population who are yet to be registered at the local civil registration office; and, difficulties in accessing and providing care and service to these OPs because they have difficulties in visiting the health facility.

In the rural settings, accessibility to healthcare seems more limited in terms of choices of health facility and available care and treatment, especially for secondary or tertiary care. The utilisation for care by OPs mostly starts at the SHPH with support from the referral system provided by the MOPH and sometimes from the local government. However, interviews revealed that if the SHPH is well equipped by sufficient medical supplies and human resources as well as activities linked to health promotion and disease prevention, the provision of care in the sub-districts will most likely be efficient and sufficient to provide heath protection, and security to OPs as social capital and networks in rural areas are still strong. Vulnerable groups of OPs (i.e. the bed-ridden, the poor OPs or those living alone or with an older spouse) tend to be more secure in rural areas because of stronger support from the community as self-help or peer support is more available.

Acceptability and unmet needs

With respect to "acceptability" of care provided to OPs, interviews found that there were some OPs who described the public health facilities to have an "elderly unfriendly environment". These are, for example, no fast track for OPs at the public hospitals,[1] no sympathy and insufficient care or a lack of respect towards OPs among some public health staffs. As reported by some OPs, as age catches on, they become more sensitive to both the verbal and physical manners of others. Doubt about quality of care and drugs prescribed at the health facilities with utilisation of benefits provided by the health scheme (in particular from the UHCS and the SSS, which are perceived by the OPs to have less premium than CSMBS) is another issue. In some cases, unmet needs (for healthcare) are not about inaccessibility to care but about inaccessibility to quality care. With long waiting times to receive care, confidence about the quality of care received, and, to some OPs, experiencing disrespectful behaviour on the part of the staff working in health facilities has led to some OPs not seeking care at public health facilities in spite of the fact that they might have health benefits offered by the health scheme they are entitled to, especially when their illness may not be serious. As mentioned in the sections titled "Outpatient care" and "Inpatient care", the percentage of older patients who did not utilise benefits from the health scheme for outpatient and inpatient care were 21.4 percent and 7.0 percent, respectively. The percentage for the inpatient care was much lower because choices of treatment methods and available health facility (for admission) were more limited and the costs of care were highly burdensome if it involved OOP payment.

In terms of vulnerability and unmet health needs, OPs who are living alone, living with a child or spouse with disabilities and abandoned persons are the most vulnerable in the community (both in economic terms and health security, e.g., poverty, housing, health status and access to services and care). These groups of OPs residing in urban areas are observed to be more vulnerable than those from the rural areas as the social and peer support in urban communities are weak. OPs with mental problems or mental disorders are another group of concern in terms of unmet health needs. Delivery of mental health services and community support for this group of OPs are found to be limited and insufficient. In some areas, there is a home visit programme for OPs with mental problems. In this programme, a medical team and a psychological doctor pay visits to the OP. However, there is a maximum of one or two visits a year since the psychological specialist is not working full-time in the area.

Affordability

Since the nationwide implementation of the UHCS in 2002, unaffordable healthcare and catastrophic health expenditure are no longer factors posing a constraint in the access of needed healthcare among Thai people, including the older population. According to the 2015 Survey on Health and Welfare, the amount of expenses paid by OPs related to the last outpatient care on average (for all types of treatment and at all health facilities), was only 130 Baht (or about $US 4.5) (median = 0 Baht) for medical fees and 132 Baht (median = 80 Baht) for travel or transportation expense. The travel expense was found to be higher among OPs living in urban areas than those residing in rural areas (mean expenses were 141 and 125 Baht and the median were 100 and 60 Baht for OPs residing in urban areas and in rural areas, respectively). On medical fees, the mean expense was found to be the highest for OPs aged 80 years and over (157 Baht), and higher for those residing in urban areas (as compared to those residing in rural areas – 188 and 90 Baht, respectively).

On the last inpatient admission, the average amount of payment for medical fees by OPs was 2,165 Baht (median = 0 Baht) and for travel expense, it was 490 Baht (median = 300 Baht). In contrast to access to outpatient care, the travel expense for inpatient care was found to be higher for OPs residing in rural areas compared with those living in urban areas (mean expenses were 511 and 455 Baht and the median was 300 and 200 Baht for OPs residing in rural areas and in urban areas, respectively). On medical fees, the mean expense was found to be the highest for OPs aged 80 years and over (3,051 Baht), and it was much higher for those living in urban areas (as compared to those residing in rural areas: 3,076 and 1,614 Baht, respectively).

Although the mean values of medical expenses for the last outpatient and inpatient treatments were 132 Baht and 2,165 Baht, respectively, the median expenses of both treatments were found to be "0" Baht – for the whole and nearly all groups of OPs when categorised by their characteristics. These findings, to some extent, are indicative of an effective financial protection made available to OPs from the existing health scheme.

Roles of the local government organisation

Health security and accessibility to healthcare of OPs in the Thai context are not only linked to the relationship between OPs and health providers. Another stakeholder outside the health service system that can play an important role in providing security and support to the older persons and facilitate their access to needed healthcare is the local government organisation (LGO). Interviews demonstrated that LGOs in the study areas provided support – both financial and non-financial – to OPs and healthcare providers in terms of an added-on budget allocated to the Sub-district Health Fund which was established in all sub-districts in the country with the initial funding from the National Health Security Office (NHSO) on a yearly basis. The fund is a financial source for supporting health-related activities of the SHPH and on-request activities by civil groups in the community including the elderly clubs. Although the support allocation targets all age-groups of the population and is not restricted to OPs, activities in health promotion and disease prevention, in particular for OPs and children, appear to be a priority.

In many events, the LGO provides places and facilities (i.e. fitness room, physical therapy place and equipment [in urban areas], outdoor exercising equipment), and sometimes health personnel [i.e. physical therapists]) for PP activities and rehabilitative services for OPs in the community. This includes also the support for "home visit" activities (i.e. transport costs for the visiting team or living toiletries for the home- or bed-bound OPs in the communities). Some LGOs organise or support the organisation of cultural events or social activities in the community (i.e. by the elderly clubs) to encourage OPs to increase their social participation to retain or improve their mental and social health. Many LGOs support an emergency car to take patients including OPs (who need transportation assistance) to the hospital via Emergency Hotline 1669 Service or on-call with fixed-schedule advanced booking.

4.5   Concluding remarks

This chapter provides an analysis the current state and situation of OPs in regard to health and access to needed healthcare and services in Thailand. The quantitative data from the country-representative secondary sources, and the qualitative data from the fieldwork in Chiangmai, are employed in the analyses and discussion.

In so far as the Thai health system is concerned, service delivery (of health promotion, disease prevention, curative care and rehabilitative care) for OPs are targeted differently to each group of OPs depending on their health status and condition. The development of long-term care for OPs, especially for those who are home- and bed-bound, has earned attention from the Thai government. The current concept is the provision of care through a combination of assistance within the family and a supporting system of healthcare and social services within the community. Community-based Older Person Home Care Volunteers have been introduced and developed, and they have been functioning in many areas in the country. More involvement and support from LGOs should be encouraged for the sustainability of the care and support system to OPs.

On health protection, the universal health coverage policy has been implemented by the Thai government since 2002. It is possible to say that all older persons in the country are entitled to or covered by at least one public health scheme among the three existing ones, which include the UHCS (80.1 percent), the CSMBS (15.8 percent) and the SSS (1.8 percent). With health benefits and protection from catastrophic health expenditure offered by the health scheme, the country's health provision has seen a success with accessibility to needed healthcare and services and also financial affordability in that healthcare at designated health facilities seems not to be a big problem to OPs. Somehow, acceptability in term of quality and safety of received care has room for improvement. Long waiting times, doubts about quality of care and drug prescribed and also (in a few cases) experiences of unfriendly manners of healthcare providers are found to be reasons for not visiting an assigned healthcare facility and utilising benefits offered by the healthcare system to some groups of elders. Apart from these, barriers in accessing healthcare among OPs include distance from home to the nearest health facility, constraints presented by the official operating times of the public health facility (in particular for inpatient care), the absence of a specialised physician in hospitals designated by health scheme and that the needed treatment was not covered by the benefit package of the available health scheme. Although findings from the fieldwork in Chiangmai that cost of transportation appeared not to be a major constraint to OPs in accessing care (especially outpatient care for minor illnesses and chronic diseases), a study conducted in many parts of the country by the World Bank had found that transportation costs and also difficulties to attain assistance from family members in order to visit a health facility when ill were the key constraints in accessing timely and relevant healthcare among OPs (Osornprasop and Sondergaard 2016). OPs who are mostly vulnerable and need attention for strengthening their health security include those who are living alone or with an older spouse, those living with family members with disabilities, abandoned OPs and those with mental health problems or difficulties.

Note

1 According to the MOPH policy, there is a "fast track" for OPs at all public health facilities. However, it is eligible only for OPs aged 70 and over.

References

Aekplakorn, W. (2009) *National Health Examination Survey (NHES) IV 2008–2009.* Nonthaburi: Health System Research Institute (HSRI), Ministry of Public Health.
——— (2014) *National Health Examination Survey (NHES) V.* Nonthaburi: Health System Research Institute (HSRI), Ministry of Public Health.
Foundation of Thai Gerontology Research and Development Institute (2012) *Situation of the Thai Elderly 2011.* Bangkok: Pongpanich-Chareonbhol Ltd.
——— (2017) *Situation of the Thai Elderly 2015.* Bangkok: Foundation of Thai Gerontology Research and Development Institute.
Institute for Population and Social Research (2017) *Mahidol Population Gazette 2017.* Nakhornprathom: Institute for Population and Social Research, Mahidol University.
National Statistical Office (2014) *The 2014 Survey of the Older Persons in Thailand.* Bangkok: Text and Journal Publication Co., Ltd.
——— (2015) *The 2015 Survey on Health and Welfare.* Bangkok: National Statistical Office, Ministry of Information and Communication Technology.
Osornprasop, S. and L.M. Sondergaard (2016) "Closing the Health Gaps for the Elderly: Promoting Health Equity and Social Inclusion in Thailand". Working Paper: AUS13326, World Bank Group, Bangkok.
Suwanrada, W. (2014) "Population Aging, Elderly Care and the Community-based Integrated Approach for Older Persons' Long-term Care System". Presentation at the ASEAN Japan Active Regional Conference, Embassy of Japan, Indonesia, June 20, 2014.
Vapattanawong, P. and P. Prasartkul (2014) "The Situation of Births During the Past Half Century". 10th Population and Social Studies: Birth and Security in Population and Society (pp. 3–22). Bangkok: Institute for Population and Social Research, Mahidol University.

5 Vietnam

*Long Thanh Giang, Phong Manh Phi
and Tham Hong Thi Pham*

5.1 Introduction

During more than twenty years of *Doi moi* (renovation) implementation, the average Gross Domestic Product (GDP) growth rate of Vietnam was about 7 percent during 1990–2015, which helped to increase GDP per capita by more than tenfold and turned the country from a poor to a low-middle-income country since 2008. Such remarkable economic growth has significantly helped to reduce national poverty rate from nearly 60 percent in early 1990 to less than 10 percent in 2015 (GSO, various years). Along with such economic achievements, health indicators of the Vietnamese people have also been improved, which are presented by such important demographic factors as higher life expectancy and very low child and maternal mortality rates. As a result, Vietnam has been moving towards an ageing population. United Nations Population Fund (UNFPA) (2011) shows that the number of old-age persons (defined as those aged 60 and over) will increase swiftly in the coming decades, and Vietnam will turn from 'ageing' to 'aged' population in less than twenty years, compared with twenty-six years in Japan and twenty-two years in Thailand.

Given the aforementioned socioeconomic successes, however, many older people are still living in poor and vulnerable conditions. Their majority are still living in rural and disadvantaged areas, where healthcare services are in crunch and low in quality (Nguyen 2010). Older people are faced with a number of health risks and new trends of illness and morbidity (Pham and Do 2009; Giang and Bui 2013), and as such adequate healthcare services are in high demand for dealing with these issues. Given the possible "getting old before getting rich" status, protecting health rights for older people is challenging.

Under such contexts, this chapter aims to provide various analyses on the current health status of older people, policies and programmes on healthcare for older people, and policy challenges as well as reform suggestions in order to adapt to a rapidly ageing population. The chapter is organised as follows: the next part provides an overview of older people's health status. The third part provides information about health systems with a focus on policies for older people. Data and research methodology are presented in the fourth part. The fourth part also analyses the findings, while the final part provides some concluding remarks.

5.2 Health status of older people in Vietnam

Figure 5.1 presents findings from a self-health assessment of OPs. About two-thirds of OPs claimed that their health was 'weak' or 'very weak'. Only 5 percent of OPs rated their health as 'good' or 'very good'.

Table 5.1 presents the detailed results of the self-health assessment of OPs in terms of age, gender and region. In terms of age, among the older age cohorts, there were more OPs who assessed their health to be not good (i.e., very poor and poor). Similarly, elderly women and OPs living in rural areas assessed poorer health status than their male and urban counterparts.

Figure 5.2 shows the symptoms that OPs experienced within thirty days prior to the interview: back pain, joint pain, dizziness and headache. These were the most common symptoms for all the age cohorts 60–69, 70–79 and 80 and over for both men and women. The percentage of OPs suffering from these symptoms increased significantly in the group aged 80 and over and among females.

Figure 5.3 shows the percentage of OPs diagnosed with diseases in terms of age, gender and living areas. Blood pressure problems, arthritis and lung problems were the most common diseases among OPs in all groups given the specific criteria above. In addition, VNAS 2011 shows that nearly 46 percent of OPs

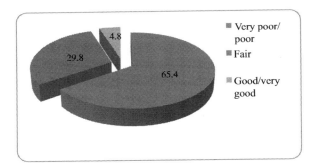

Figure 5.1 OPs' self-assessment on their current health status
Source: Vietnam Aging Survey (VNAS) 2011

Table 5.1 Self-assessment of health status by population (percent)

	Total	Age			Sex		Ethnicity	
		60–69	*70–79*	*80+*	*Male*	*Female*	*Kinh*	*Ethnic minorities*
Very weak	10.1	5.0	13.0	15.9	8.8	10.9	8.8	10.7
Weakness	55.3	53.4	55.4	58.9	50.4	58.6	46.5	59.3
Normal	29.8	35.3	27.9	21.5	34.3	26.8	38.6	25.8
Good	4.4	5.9	3.1	3.3	6.1	3.2	5.5	3.8
Very good	0.4	0.4	0.6	0.4	0.4	0.5	0.6	0.4

Source: Vietnam Aging Survey (VNAS) 2011

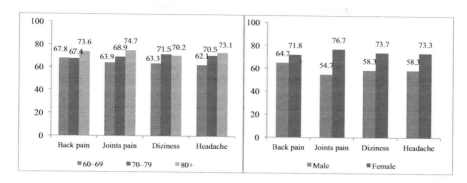

Figure 5.2 Symptoms that OPs had in the last thirty days prior to the date of interview
Source: Vietnam Aging Survey (VNAS) 2011

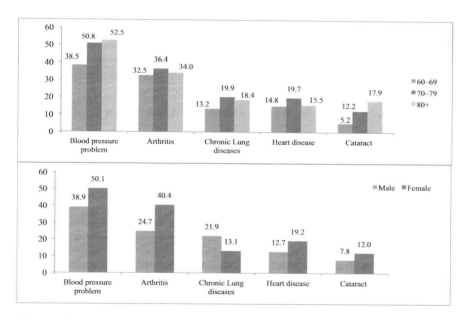

Figure 5.3 Percentage of older people being diagnosed with diseases
Source: Vietnam Aging Survey (VNAS) 2011

were diagnosed with high blood pressure and 34 percent were diagnosed with arthritis, and the percentage suffering with these diseases increased with age. Other diseases such as cardiovascular disease, dental problems, bronchitis and chronic lung disease are the diseases that OPs often suffered from, which accounts for about 20 percent. The proportion of elderly women suffering from high blood pressure, arthritis and heart diseases was higher than for elderly men. A higher percentage of OPs living in rural areas were found to be suffering from bronchitis and chronic lung diseases compared with those living in urban areas.

Figures 5.4–5.6 show the percentage of OPs in terms of age and gender facing difficulties with daily activities, as well as having problems with vision and hearing.

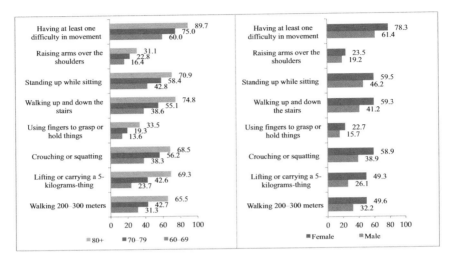

Figure 5.4 Percentage of older people having difficulties with movements

Source: Vietnam Aging Survey (VNAS) 2011

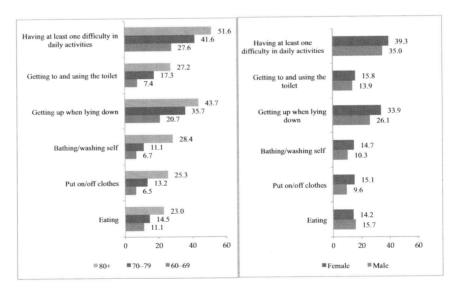

Figure 5.5 Percentage of the elderly having difficulties with daily activities

Source: Vietnam Aging Survey (VNAS) 2011

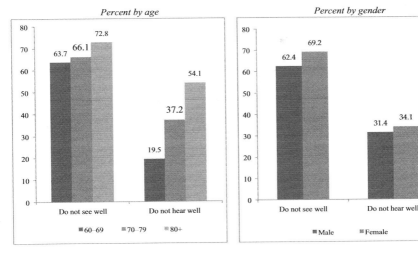

Figure 5.6 Percentage of the elderly having difficulties with vision and hearing
Source: Vietnam Aging Survey (VNAS) 2011

Generally, difficulties increased with age, and female OPs were found to have more difficulties with movement, daily activities, vision and hearing than male OPs.

5.3 Healthcare systems and policies focusing on older people

5.3.1 *The law on the elderly and other related laws and regulations*

This law was approved by the National Assembly on 23 November 2009. It stipulates the rights to healthcare of OPs. There are two areas: (a) primary healthcare at home, and (b) medical examination and treatment at health facilities. Primary healthcare for OPs is specified in Article 13. According to this Article, commune health stations act as primary health facilities responsible for managing the health of OPs through health communication and education, the establishment of health records of OPs, the provision of health services within their level of technical service capacity and the collaboration among upper-level health facilities to organise routine health check-ups for OPs. For OPs without caregivers and who have serious illnesses and are unable to visit health facilities, commune health stations are responsible for sending staff to the home of the OP for medical examination/treatment and Commune People's Committees are responsible for bringing such OPs to health facilities at the request of commune health stations. The government also encourages other organisations and individuals to provide medical examinations and treatment for OPs in their home.

Article 12 of the Law provides the prioritisation of healthcare for OPs. In the law, people aged 80 and over are entitled to receive medical examination and treatment before other patients; now the eligibility age has been changed to 75 as regulated in the MOH's Decision No. 2413/BYT-KCB dated 26 April 2013. Along with this provision, OPs are provided with suitable beds for inpatient treatments in a geriatric department or in beds specifically designated for OPs in hospitals. After the treatment of acute symptoms in a hospital setting, OPs will receive rehabilitation services and guidance on how to maintain follow-up treatment and care at home.

In addition, the law stipulates the rights of OPs to health insurance and the responsibilities of the MOH. OPs account for a large proportion of the population with disabilities. Specifically, the Law on Persons with Disabilities covers the right to rehabilitation among OPs (Law No. 51/2010/QH12, dated 17 June 2010).

5.3.2 The Health Insurance Law

Along with the Law on the Elderly, the Health Insurance Law stipulates the rights of OPs to health insurance. In particular, for those aged 80 and over, their health insurance premiums are paid either by the Vietnam Social Security (VSS) or by the state budget. For those aged 60–79, some groups (i.e. pensioners, the poor without family members who are obliged to provide support, people with meritorious services and people with disabilities living on monthly social assistance payment) will receive their health insurance premiums paid by VSS or by the state budget, while the rest in that age group have to pay the health insurance premiums by themselves. Specifically, for poor OPs who do not have family members providing care towards them, the insurance premiums are to be paid by the family caregivers. For OPs under age 80 entitled to survivor allowances from VSS, they are expected to pay premiums to obtain voluntary health insurance from their survivor allowance, while other groups like the non-poor, people without meritorious services, non-pensioners and people without disabilities are expected to pay health insurance premiums by themselves. These groups are likely not to participate in health insurance, or to participate in health insurance only when they have a disease, leading to adverse selection in health insurance. According to this Law, older persons participating in health insurance under most of the above-mentioned groups shall pay a co-payment rate of 20 percent, while the remaining 80 percent is covered by health insurance. OPs who are poor, or who are social policy beneficiaries, shall be completely covered by healthcare costs provided by health insurance. Upon reaching age 80, the co-payment rate falls to 5 percent. However, the health insurance reimbursement rate will be reduced if OPs bypass lower-level facilities to use services at higher levels without a referral.

5.3.3 Decision 1781/QĐ-TTg on national plan of actions for older people in 2012–2020

This was issued by the Prime Minister on 22 November 2012. In Section IV, Article 2 stipulates various provisions and activities on healthcare for OPs, including education and training on knowledge and skills for OPs and their families in self-care; the establishment of geriatric departments at district and province-level health facilities; the establishment of networks for healthcare and rehabilitation for OPs; and the integration of healthcare for OPs into a variety of preventive care; and the establishment of research projects for OP's health and training activities for social workers and volunteers in providing care towards OPs.

5.3.4 Decree 136/2013/NĐCP and inter-circular 29/2014/TTLT-BLĐTBXH-BTC

Decree 136 was issued on 21 October 2013 with a number of regulations on social assistance, while Inter-Circular 29/2014/TTLT-BLĐTBXH-BTC was issued on 24 October 2013 to guide the implementation of Decree 136. In conformity with the Law on the Elderly, the decree stipulates the rights to health-care for OPs and, in particular, in providing health insurance. Under this decree, OPs without familial support who have a disability, are aged 80 and over, and are lacking social and health insurance will be provided free health insurance.

5.3.5 Circular 35/TT-BYT

This circular, issued on 15 October 2011, guides healthcare for OPs. In particular, the circular stipulates activities for community-based healthcare for OPs (such as providing regular health checkups for OPs at least once a year, guiding OPs in preventive, curative and self-care, and community-based management of chronic diseases).

5.4 Assessments of health security among older people in Vietnam

5.4.1 Methods

In order to provide assessments of health rights to older people in Vietnam, this chapter uses both quantitative and qualitative approaches. In regard to the quantitative approach adopted in the following discussion, the chapter uses various secondary, nationally-representative data such as statistics of OPs and their use of healthcare services and related issues. In order to complement the quantitative analyses with further illustrative descriptions, the discussion also uses qualitative data through field surveys.

Quantitative approach

VIETNAM HOUSEHOLD LIVING STANDARD SURVEY (VHLSS)

To pursue the objectives, the authors utilised the Vietnam Household Living Standard Survey (VHLSS) from 2002 to 2014. The survey is conducted every

two years by the General Statistics Office (GSO). Although the survey is conducted at the household level, it includes a number of individual characteristics
such as age, gender, relationship to the household head, marital status, work
status and educational attainment. Such data enabled the authors to identify an
elderly person (aged 60 and over) and an elderly household (which includes at
least one elderly person).

At the household level, the survey provides information on the sources of
income, household expenditure, ownership of consumer durables, business and
agricultural activities, poverty incidence, participation in poverty alleviation
programmes, social insurance, wealth and housing conditions. In regard to
health status and financing for healthcare services to OPs, VHLSS had a number
of questions on participation in the social health insurance, utilisation of social
health insurance (SHI) in healthcare services and out-of-pocket (OOP) payments
for healthcare. However, VHLSS did not provide detailed diseases of OPs and
thus, the authors could not determine the treatment costs for their diseases.

VIETNAM AGING SURVEY (VNAS) IN 2011

In order to provide more detailed analyses on such important information such
as health status and the utilisation of healthcare services for OPs which were
not provided in the VHLSS, this chapter also utilised data from the Vietnam
Aging Survey (VNAS). The VNAS, conducted in late 2011, was the first-ever
nationally representative survey on persons aged 50 and over in Vietnam. This
survey was designed and sampled by using the data from the Population and
Housing Census in 2009. Eligible interviewees were chosen by multi-stage
sampling method. Using the probability proportional to size (PPS) method,
more than 4,000 people aged 50 and over from 200 communes in twelve
provinces representing six ecological regions in Vietnam were defined and surveyed. In this chapter, the sample size comprised 2,789 people aged 60 and
over, of which 1,683 were females and 1,106 were males; 2,050 lived in rural
areas, while 739 lived in urban areas.

The VNAS provided individual and household information on OPs such as
education, marital status, work status, living conditions, health conditions and
roles and contributions of OPs to their families (VWU 2012). In regard to
health status, utilisation of healthcare services and financial sources for the
healthcare of OPs, VNAS provided detailed information about OPs' current
diagnosed diseases, participation in the social health insurance programme,
satisfaction with the provided healthcare services at different levels of care and
providers of finance for healthcare.

SURVEY ON SHI-PAID HEALTHCARE SERVICES BY MINISTRY OF HEALTH (MOH)
AND HEALTH AND FINANCE GOVERNANCE (HFG) PROJECT

Under the collaboration between USAID (United States Agency for International
Development), MOH and VSS in 2015, MOH and the HFG (Health and Finance

Governance) project conducted a survey to collect data on SHI-paid healthcare services in some provinces/cities. In order to have representative data for the whole country, the studied provinces/cities were selected using the following provincial statistical indictors related to healthcare and health insurance in 2014: (a) population (persons); (b) health infrastructure: number of hospitals; number of regional health facilities; number of commune health centres (CHCs) and equivalent; number of beds in hospitals; number of beds in regional health facilities; and number of beds in CHCs and equivalent; (c) human resources: number of doctors; number of nurses; and, number of midwives. All statistical indicators for each district in each province/city were compared to that province/city's averages. Indicators being equal or higher than the averages were given 1 point, while those being lower than the averages were given 0 points. At the end, six provinces/cities were chosen for six regions which included: Hoa Binh (representing for Northern Mountainous and Midlands Region), Ha Noi (representing for Red River Delta), Binh Dinh (representing for Central Coastal Region), Gia Lai (representing for Central Highlands), Ho Chi Minh City (representing for Southeast Region) and Dong Thap (representing for Mekong River Delta).

The collected data included information about patients' age, sex, diseases coded according to international code of disease (ICD), type of treatments (inpatient, outpatient), number of technical services provided to patients and their respective costs, total cost of healthcare services and total cost paid by SHI. With this information, the authors could define elderly patients (those aged 60 and over) along with their respective diseases, provided services and costs. This dataset provided further details about health status and costs of healthcare services for OPs compared to those from VHLSS and VNAS.

Combining these datasets helped provide a more comprehensive picture of the health status, healthcare services and costs for OPs, as well as costs covered by SHI. However, it is also worth noting that representative levels for older populations in these datasets were different, so the authors had to be careful when interpreting the results. These datasets should be considered to be complementary rather than comparative to each other.

Qualitative approach

In order to provide additional information for the quantitative analyses, this chapter also utilises information from the qualitative field surveys at: (a) central-level organisations, including the Vietnam Association of the Elderly (VAE) and the Vietnam National Committee on Ageing (VNCA) as they had monitored the implementation of healthcare policies for OPs; and (b) local authorities and local OPs from two provinces, i.e., Hai Duong in the north, and Ben Tre in the south, because these provinces were among those with the highest ageing indices in the Red River Delta and the Mekong River Delta, respectively. Data from the Population and Housing Census in 2009 show that the proportion of OPs in the population in Hai Duong was 12 percent and in Ben Tre was 10.9 percent, and the ageing index in Hai Duong and Ben Tre in 2009 was 54 and 48, respectively. It is estimated that the proportion of OPs in Hai Duong and Ben Tre will increase to 14.6 percent and 14.5 percent in 2019, and to 20.2 percent and 21.9 percent in 2029 (GSO 2011).

In each province, the authors chose a district with the highest proportion of OPs. In each chosen district, we selected two communes with different economic situations – one would be considered poor and the other not poor. In each district and commune, the authors conducted qualitative surveys with two main approaches: Focus Group Discussions (FGDs) and In-Depth Interviews (IDIs).

In each commune, FGDs with OPs involved the participation of six persons aged 60–69 (three men and three women); six persons aged 70–79 (three men and three women); and four persons aged 80 and over (two men and two women). In total, in each district/province, data was collected from sixteen OPs.

For the IDIs with OPs, for each age group, there were two persons (one man and one woman) who participated in the study; in each district/province, six IDIs were conducted with six OPs. In addition, the authors conducted FGDs with local authorities, including commune administrators, representatives from local unions for women, youth, farmers, veterans, father front and elderly associations. The authors conducted one FGD for each commune and with a total of two FGDs for these persons in one province. To explore the current situation of healthcare service provision, IDIs were conducted with two heads of commune health stations in each province.

After the data collection stage was completed, all the recorded tapes were transcribed into written text. All hand-written notes made during the interviews and the discussions were typed and then cleaned up to improve readability and comprehension.

Table 5.2 summarises the sample size for the qualitative surveys using FGD and IDI.

Table 5.2 Sample sizes for qualitative surveys

No.	Target group	Central level		Local level		Total
		FGD	*IDI*	*FGD*	*IDI*	
				2 prov./2 dist./ 4 communes	*2 prov./2 dist./ 4 communes*	
1	Central authorities	0	2	–	–	–
2	Older persons	–	–	32	12	44
3	Local authorities	–	–	0	4	4
4	Local health providers	–	–	0	4	4
	Total	*0*	*2*	*32*	*20*	*52*

5.4.2 Key findings on health security among older people in Vietnam

Accessibility

Table 5.3 shows the physical accessibility of OPs to health services over the period 2002–2008, captured by the percentage of OPs living in a commune with a health centre and the distance from their village to the nearest hospital. It was found that almost every commune has one health centre, which helps increase accessibility among OPs to healthcare services. In terms of distance to the nearest hospital, however, although gaps have been narrowed, there have been significant differences between OP groups among those living in the poorer and difficult geographic areas (such as ethnic minority people, those living in the Northwest and Central Highlands and those living in poor households) compared with those who do not.

In the mountainous areas, it is very difficult for people to reach commune health stations, especially in the rainy seasons. It is even impossible for older people who have difficulties in movement. In urban and plain areas, it is

Table 5.3 Physical accessibility to healthcare services of older people, 2002–2008

Individual groups	Percent elderly living in a commune with a health centre				Distance from village to the nearest hospital (km)			
	2002	2004	2006	2008	2002	2004	2006	2008
All	97.2	99.3	98.8	99.3	10.4	6.6	6.6	7.4
Ethnicity								
Kinh/Hoa	97.1	99.2	98.8	99.4	9.2	6.3	6.1	7.0
Ethnic minorities	98.3	99.7	98.5	98.5	17.1	8.3	8.9	10.0
Region								
Red River Delta	94.4	99.9	99.3	100.0	6.7	5.5	5.6	6.2
North East	96.3	100.0	99.8	99.3	12.7	7.6	7.8	8.0
North West	100.0	98.5	100.0	100.0	18.7	10.2	9.1	10.6
North Central Coast	99.6	99.2	100.0	100.0	9.6	7.5	7.0	8.2
South Central Coast	99.6	99.4	99.3	98.4	8.4	6.0	8.1	8.1
Central Highlands	96.7	97.4	96.6	98.3	15.2	7.8	7.4	10.7
South East	99.7	99.7	99.3	99.5	13.5	6.9	4.4	6.7
Mekong River Delta	97.4	98.5	96.7	98.3	11.0	6.1	6.2	6.6
Poor/Non-Poor household								
Non-Poor	96.8	99.2	98.6	99.4	9.3	6.2	6.3	7.2
Poor	98.2	99.4	99.3	99.0	12.5	7.8	7.4	8.3

Source: Nguyen and Giang (2012), calculations using VHLSS 2002, 2004, 2006 and 2008

easier with various means of transportation, but in these difficult areas no transport means that sometimes it is difficult for patients to access healthcare services.

(IDI, a representative from the
Vietnam Association of the Elderly)

Poor older people usually live in rural and remote areas where the infrastructure has not been developed. As such, it usually takes time for them to access the commune health stations. It is even more time-consuming to reach district and provincial health facilities.

(IDI, a representative from the
Vietnam National Committee on Ageing)

Table 5.4 shows the utilisation rates of healthcare services at the different types of health facilities by OPs with various individual and household characteristics. In general, more than 50 percent of OPs used healthcare services at the district level and above. Older people having SHI tended to have higher utilisation rates than those who did not have SHI. More importantly, older people without SHI had much higher rates of using different healthcare services (such as traditional medical doctors and private care) than those with SHI. In terms of the ethnicity of the household head, OPs living in households headed by Kinh people had much higher rates of using health facilities at the district level and above than those living in households headed by ethnic minorities, while the pattern was the reverse at the commune health stations. Similar trends were also observed among older people living in urban and rural areas: those living in urban areas had much lower rates of using commune health stations but much higher rates of using health facilities at the district level and above than did those living in rural areas. Older people living in poor households also had higher rates of using commune health stations than those not living in poor households, and the patterns were the reverse among those using the health facilities at the district level and above. By per capita expenditure quintile, the authors found similar trends, as in poverty status of older people's households.

We usually visit commune health stations first to know our health status. If treatments are needed, we ask for a referral to the district- or provincial-level health facilities. Higher levels of care surely provide better treatment, but also have high costs.

(FGD, a group aged 60–69, Ben Tre province)

Articulating commune and district levels for healthcare gives us convenient access to health services. However, moving to provincial and central levels is usually costly, especially for inpatient treatments.

(FGD, a group aged 70–79, Hai Duong province)

Table 5.4 Distribution of healthcare facilities accessed by older people, 2014

	Commune Health Station	District health facility	Provincial and central health facility	State hospital	Other hospital	Private health facility	Other	Total
Total	*12.77*	*30.24*	*21.11*	*1.55*	*0.1*	*11.27*	*22.96*	*100*
Had SHI card?								
Yes	13.50	32.76	22.85	1.36	0.14	9.36	20.03	100
No	10.82	23.54	16.49	2.07	0.00	16.34	30.74	100
Ethnicity of household head								
Kinh	11.11	30.01	22.29	1.66	0.09	11.81	23.03	100
Ethnic minority	27.75	32.33	10.45	0.58	6.31	0.18	22.40	100
Living area								
Urban	5.72	28.66	31.78	3.40	0.20	13.74	16.50	100
Rural	16.27	31.03	15.80	0.63	0.06	10.03	26.18	100
Household poverty								
Poor	31.02	26.73	8.63	0.12	0.15	6.63	26.72	100
Non-poor	10.22	30.73	22.85	1.75	0.10	11.91	22.44	100
Household per capita expenditure quintile								
Poorest	27.92	29.11	9.99	0.09	0.11	8.06	24.72	100
Near poor	15.37	29.21	12.84	1.40	0.00	10.11	31.07	100
Middle	13.12	34.32	17.05	0.56	0.00	10.41	24.54	100
Near rich	6.89	30.57	26.87	2.85	0.09	14.15	18.58	100
Richest	4.53	27.99	34.94	2.45	0.29	12.77	17.03	100

Source: Own calculations, using VHLSS 2014

Table 5.5 Social Health Insurance participation rate of older people, 2006–2014

	2006	2010	2014
Total	**43.5**	**67.5**	**75.0**
Age group			
60–69	45.20	58.14	71.9
70–79	42.38	61.60	76.8
80+	40.46	59.23	80.2
Sex			
Female	41.33	64.2	75.5
Male	46.49	72.1	74.3
Ethnicity of household head			
Kinh	42.56	66.0	73.4
Ethnic minority	53.92	80.3	89.5
Living area			
Urban	39.94	65.7	73.4
Rural	41.68	71.3	78.1
Household poverty status			
Non-poor	42.67	66.2	74.1
Poor	50.56	77.7	82.2

Source: Giang, Pham and Pham (2016), using VHLSS 2006, 2010 and 2014

Another important aspect is accessibility to SHI, which is a crucial channel to make healthcare services accessible to OPs is financing. Table 5.5 describes rates of participation in SHI by various groups of OPs. Generally, the participation rate of the older population has increased significantly and reached 75 percent in 2014. In terms of age group, the oldest of the OPs had the fastest increase in coverage. As discussed earlier, such results showed efficiency of various policies and programmes in promoting and supporting OPs in participating in the SHI scheme. In terms of sex, no significant difference between male and female OPs was observed. An encouraging result was that the participation rate of ethnic minority OPs increased substantially and reached about 90 percent in 2014. This resulted from the policy providing free health insurance to ethnic minority people in recent years. Participation rates of urban and rural older people increased significantly, but the former had a higher rate of participation than did the latter. There have been a variety of reasons, but the most frequently mentioned was that those living in rural areas had low affordability, and regulations on household-based participation are a barrier, especially for those living in large households. The participation rate of older people living in poor households was higher than those living in non-poor households. This also resulted from the rapid expansion of SHI to poor people in recent years.

Table 5.6 shows utilisation rates of health services in the older population by level of care and type of treatment. For outpatient services, calculations

Table 5.6 Utilisation rates for healthcare by level of care, 2014

	Central level or equivalent	*Provincial level or equivalent*	*District level or equivalent*	*Commune level or equivalent*
Outpatient visit (times/year)	2.69	6.06	5.77	7.20
Inpatient admission (times/year)	1.16	1.61	1.56	1.22
Total (times/ year)	2.21	4.84	5.14	7.14

Source: Own calculations, using data collected by MOH and HFG in 2015

from VHLSS 2014 show that, on average, an older person had three visits per year for outpatient services. In term of age group, there were no differences among those with SHI, but there were significant differences among those without SHI, in that more elderly tended to have higher number of visits than younger groups. These observations could be elucidated by the fact that those aged 60–69 had both adverse selection (if those holding SHI used services more than needed) and moral hazard (those holding SHI tended to be less healthy than those without SHI). It is difficult to explain the finding that those aged 70–79 and 80 and over without SHI tended to have higher outpatient visits than those with SHI.

For inpatient services, higher costs prevent access to services. However, once health status risks life, households usually seek solutions to save their members, including OPs. Calculations also indicate that, among those having SHI, more OPs tended to have higher inpatient admissions than younger persons. Among those without SHI, however, there was no difference in inpatient admissions between those aged 80 and over and those aged 70–79, implying that financial constraints affected more elderly in the utilisation of inpatient services.

Frequency for outpatient services reduced gradually from the commune to central levels, while that for inpatient admission was highest at the provincial level, followed by the district level. According to Giang et al. (2016), at all levels of care, OPs had about two to four times greater health service utilisation than younger people; in contrast, they generally had about two times that of younger persons in inpatient services, while for the outpatient services older people's frequency of utilisation was highest at the CHCs (on average, seven times per annum); and it was about four times higher than that for the younger population (on average, 1.88 times per annum).

Affordability

Table 5.7 shows the results for number of inpatient admissions and outpatient visits and their respective total cost, and average cost for older people by age and sex. In general, the total number of outpatient visits were about eight to

Table 5.7 Related indicators for older persons' inpatient admissions and outpatient visits, 2014

	Male			Female		
	60–69	70–79	80+	60–69	70–79	80+
Inpatient services						
Number of admissions	133,723	99,061	66,061	156,097	124,040	84,245
Total cost (VND million)	654,672	474,630	313,116	604,518	475,031	348,018
Average cost (VND million)	4.90	4.79	4.74	3.87	3.83	4.13
Outpatient services						
Number of admissions	1,732,697	1,016,089	482,064	2,538,687	1,484,307	627,095
Total cost (VND million)	447,145	259,256	119,074	641,508	375,953	144,537
Average cost (VND million)	0.26	0.26	0.25	0.25	0.25	0.23

Source: Giang et al. (2016), using data from MOH and HFG in 2015

13 times higher than that for inpatient admissions. In contrast, however, the average cost per one inpatient admission was about 12–18 times higher than that for one outpatient visit. Such contrasting numbers were indicated by the fact that inpatient admissions and outpatient visits were different in terms of costs for drugs and technical services. For outpatient visits, there were no differences between male and female OPs in average cost (about VND 0.23 to VND 0.26 million); for inpatient admissions, there were significant differences across all age groups, in which male OPs incurred higher costs than females. Calculations for cost components show that such sex differences were mostly a result of large differences in costs for drugs and technical services, especially at the district and provicial health facilities.

Table 5.8 lists five disease groups of OPs which have the highest costs covered by SHI. In general, the total cost for these five disease groups accounted for 75 percent of the total cost of all 22 groups defined in ICD-10. In both inpatient and outpatient services, SHI covered about 85 percent of the total cost for older patients. SHI covered 85 percent of the total costs for disease groups with very high costs for inpatient services (such as neoplasms and diseases of the circulatory system) and outpatient services (such as diseases of the circulatory system and diseases of the musculoskeletal system and connective tissue).

Table 5.8 Five most costly disease groups of older people paid by Social Health Insurance, 2014

ICD	Total cost (VND million)	Percent total cost	Percent cumulative	Percent paid by SHI
Inpatient				**84.83**
1 Neoplasms	873,686	22.49	22.49	86.63
2 Diseases of the circulatory system	835,238	21.50	43.98	86.30
3 Diseases of the respiratory system	557,049	14.34	58.32	88.87
4 Diseases of the eye and adnexa	294,754	7.59	65.90	68.45
5 Diseases of the digestive system	259,029	6.67	72.57	86.09
6 Other disease groups	1,065,873	27.43	100.00	84.32
Total cost	*3,885,629*	*100.00*	*100.00*	
Outpatient				**86.03**
1 Diseases of the circulatory system	960,554	36.85	36.85	86.70
2 Endocrine, nutritional and metabolic diseases	457,621	17.56	54.41	87.85
3 Diseases of the musculoskeletal system and connective tissue	241,139	9.25	63.66	82.96
4 Diseases of the respiratory system	194,728	7.47	71.14	84.47
5 Diseases of the digestive system	164,169	6.30	77.44	83.80
6 Other disease groups	588,116	22.56	100.00	85.48
Total cost	*2,606,327*	*100.00*	*100.00*	

Source: Giang et al. (2016), using data from MOH and HFG in 2015

Older people usually have multiple diseases and most of them are chronic. Having health insurance helps reduce costs of care. But it depends on which health facility an older person has check-ups and receives treatment.

(IDI, a commune health centre head, Ben Tre province)

Health insurance now plays a greater role in covering costs of healthcare, especially for very advanced age persons.

(IDI, a representative of VAE)

Although SHI aims to provide financial protection to the insured patients, Table 5.9 shows that for those aged less than 80, SHI holders had lower

Table 5.9 Out-of-pocket payments for healthcare services by Social Health Insurance holding status, 2014

	Older people with SHI		Older people without SHI	
Outpatient	*Average number of visits (times)*	*Average OOP per visit (VND 1,000)*	*Average number of visits (times)*	*Average OOP per visit (VND 1,000)*
Total	3.08	970.52	2.90	1,237.61
Age group				
60–69	3.15	966.11	2.58	1,070.65
70–79	3.06	1,055.69	3.22	1,245.89
80+	2.95	864.24	3.49	1,876.27
Inpatient	*Average number of admissions (times)*	*Average OOP per admission (VND 1,000)*	*Average number of admissions (times)*	*Average OOP per admission (VND 1,000)*
Total	0.34	4,361.24	0.27	6,596.80
Age group				
60–69	0.29	4,771.44	0.25	5,960.53
70–79	0.34	4,381.61	0.30	10,880.12
80+	0.45	3,662.06	0.29	2,935.43

Source: Own calculations, using VHLSS 2014

OOP payments than did SHI non-holders; but for those aged 80 and over, SHI holders had half of OOP payments lower than did SHI non-holders. The average OOP payments per year for outpatient services was about VND 1–2 million, and thus it could be seen that the amount is not significantly high. The co-payment for OPs with SHI was about VND 4 million per annum and it did not increase, although the average number of IP admissions or OP visits increased. For the SHI non-holders, those aged 70–79 had very high OOP payments, which were about twice that of SHI holders. For SHI non-holders aged 80 and over, the OOP payments was lower and it was because of the fact that they used fewer services.

It is financially burdensome for OPs without health insurance to access healthcare as costs of care are increasing. I know some cases of OPs who did not go to any health facilities to receive treatment although they had serious diseases. This was because they did not have health insurance and could not afford costly services.

(IDI, a representative of VNCA)

Although health insurance is still limited in covering costs, it helps reduce out-of-pocket payments for OPs, particularly those with chronic diseases.

(IDI, a commune health centre head,
Hai Duong province)

Table 5.10 Affordability of elderly households for healthcare services, 2014

	With SHI				Without SHI			
	Yes, enough	Yes, but not enough	Unaffordable	Total	Yes, enough	Yes, but not enough	Unaffordable	Total
Total	96.12	2.80	1.09	100	97.83	1.90	0.27	100
Ethnicity of household head								
Kinh	96.48	2.67	0.84	100	97.74	1.98	0.28	100
Ethnic minority	93.32	3.75	2.93	100	100	0.00	0.00	100
Living area								
Urban	98.14	1.36	0.50	100	98.87	1.13	0.00	100
Rural	94.97	3.61	1.42	100	97.36	2.25	0.39	100
Poverty status of household								
Poor	90.04	5.43	4.53	100	97.30	2.70	0.00	100
Non-poor	97.00	2.42	0.58	100	97.87	1.83	0.30	100
Household per capita expenditure quintile								
Poorest	90.77	5.04	4.18	100	96.97	3.03	0.00	100
Near poor	95.83	3.56	0.61	100	98.22	1.78	0.00	100
Middle	97.21	2.17	0.62	100	96.29	2.59	1.11	100
Near rich	97.05	2.17	0.77	100	97.89	2.11	0.00	100
Richest	98.20	1.80	0.00	100	100	0.00	0.00	100

Source: Own calculations, using VHLSS 2014

On self-assessed affordability for healthcare by households with older people, Table 5.10 compares OPs with SHI and those without SHI in the past 12 months by their individual and household characteristics. In general, for both OPs with and without SHI, their households' affordability was quite high (about 96–97 percent), but there were differences between groups of OPs. For instance, for OPs living in urban areas – whether they had SHI or not – the numbers who found healthcare to be 'affordable' were higher than their rural counterparts. Similarly, for poverty status and for per capita expenditure quintiles, OPs who were non-poor or at a higher quintile usually had higher rates of affordability than their poor and lower quintile counterparts.

In addition to this, Vietnam Women Union (VWU) (2012) with data from VNAS 2011 found that household financial status had a significant impact on health risks and health status that, in turn, affected financing-seeking behaviours. About 10 percent of OPs had savings, and 68 percent said that they saved for precaution (such as payments for healthcare services). The rate of elderly households with debt because of health problems was 13.8 percent. Data from VNAS 2011 show that the rate of OPs who answered "Who was the major payer for your healthcare?" was 37.62 percent for sons, 17.29 percent for daughters, 17.41 percent for themselves and 10.11 percent for spouses, while it was small for other groups of people. About 30.3 percent of OPs said that SHI was the main source of financing for their healthcare.

> I do not have enough money for treatments even though I have health insurance. My children usually pay for the additional costs.
>
> (An older woman, FGD in Hai Duong province)

> For simple diseases, it is fine with health insurance. However, we cannot afford inpatient care for chronic diseases if we have to be referred to the provincial or central hospitals. Costs are high and are increasing.
>
> (An older man, FGD in Ben Tre province)

Availability

There are vast differences between OP groups who receive healthcare when needed. Table 5.11 shows the percentage of the sick or injured OPs who are in need of treatment but could not receive healthcare services. On average, about 55 percent of OPs did not get treatment when they needed it, and the proportions for the elderly and those living in rural areas were higher than their younger and urban counterparts, respectively. Among the reasons for not receiving healthcare, "Not enough money for treatment" was the majority reason, followed by "No one to take to treatment" and "Think that I am not sick enough". For all these main reasons, there were significant differences among OPs in terms of age groups and living areas; among them, the numbers of the elderly and those living in rural areas were higher compared to the younger age people and those living in the rural areas.

> Health services are available to all OPs, but adequate and affordable services are limited among those with serious diseases and who require urgent treatment and highly technical healthcare services as they are really costly.
>
> (IDI with representative from VAE)

> If I am sick enough, I do not want to disturb children or grandchildren to take me to hospital, because it sometimes takes a whole day to get all the procedures done. A lot of costs arise such as accommodation and transportation along with the treatments.
>
> (FGD with older group aged 80 and over, Ben Tre province)

Acceptability

In terms of acceptability, data from VNAS 2011 showed that the majority of respondents were satisfied with the quality of healthcare they received on their last visit. Figure 5.7 (left panel) shows that 84 percent of OPs were satisfied with the healthcare services in the past twelve months. Figure 5.7 (right panel) indicates that 80 percent of OPs were very satisfied or satisfied with their received healthcare services at the district and provincial health facilities, but it was still lower than that for private health facilities, CHCs and central health facilities.

Table 5.11 Percent of sick/injured older people in need of treatment but did not receive, and reason

	Total	Age			Area	
		60–69	70–79	80+	Urban	Rural
Proportion of having access to treatment but no treatment (percent)	54.9	55.8	47.3	60.6	58.5	53.0
Reasons for no treatment (percent by reason)						
• Not enough money for treatment	52.5	68.0	30.6	50.2	47.4	55.4
• No one to pay for treatment	–	–	–	–	–	–
• No one to take to treatment	11.5	0.9	14.7	21.7	0.0	18.1
• No transportation available	2.7	0.0	1.3	6.7	0.0	4.2
• Could not afford transportation costs	0.1	0.0	0.0	0.1	0.0	0.1
• Do not know where to go	–	–	–	–	–	–
• Too far to go	1.3	2.8	0.0	0.6	0.0	2.1
• Too shy to ask for help	1.6	0.0	4.6	1.4	0.0	2.6
• Do not want to go for help	3.9	0.0	15.5	0.0	0.0	6.1
• Previously treated badly	2.6	2.5	0.0	4.7	0.0	4.1
• Tried but being denied	–	–	–	–	–	–
• Could not take time off work or had other	1.1	2.6	0.0	0.0	0.0	1.6
• Think that not sick enough	11.8	2.9	24.4	13.2	26.5	3.4
• Other	10.9	20.3	8.9	1.4	26.1	2.3
Total	100	100	100	100	100	100

Source: VWU (2012)

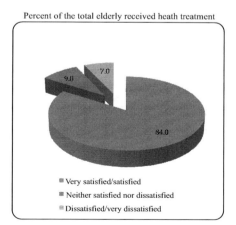

Percent of the total elderly received heath treatment

■ Very satisfied/satisfied
■ Neither satisfied nor dissatisfied
■ Dissatisfied/very dissatisfied

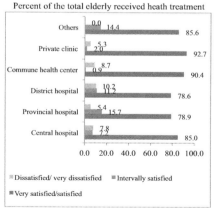

Percent of the total elderly received heath treatment

▨ Dissatisfied/ very dissatisfied   ■ Intervally satisfied
■ Very satisfied/satisfied

Figure 5.7 Older people's satisfaction with the received healthcare services
Source: VWU (2012)

Table 5.12 shows details about satisfaction among OPs with their received healthcare services by age, sex, living area and living region. Those more advanced in age, female and rural OPs tended to report higher rates of being 'very satisfied' or 'satisfied' than their younger, male and urban counterparts. By level of care, it is noteworthy that the satisfaction rate of OPs with CHCs was significantly high (90.4 percent), but their utilisation rate of CHCs was quite low, at only 8.8 percent (Table 5.13).

Although the overall satisfaction with health facilities was quite high, there were various concerns among OPs in accessing services along with bearing costs at the different health facilities.

> I usually use commune health stations only for simple diseases. When I have more serious diseases, I use district or provincial hospitals, and even sometimes central hospitals. But costs are much higher in upper-level facilities, and more than that I have to wait for a long time to get the help I need.
>
> (FGD, Hai Duong province)

Table 5.12 Satisfaction levels with received healthcare services

	Total	Age			Sex		Area		Region		
		60–69	70–79	80+	Male	Female	Urban	Rural	North	Central	South
(Very) satisfied	84.0	83.3	84.0	85.4	72.7	90.0	80.3	85.5	77.4	83.1	91.4
Normal	9.0	11.5	5.1	11.3	14.4	6.1	8.5	9.1	12.2	9.4	5.4
(Very) dissatisfied	7.0	5.2	10.9	3.3	12.9	3.9	11.2	5.4	10.4	7.5	3.2
Total	100	100	100	100	100	100	100	100	100	100	100

Source: VWU (2012)

Table 5.13 Percent satisfied with received healthcare services by type of health facility

	(Very) satisfied	Normal	(Very) dissatisfied	Total
Central health facilities	85.0	7.2	7.8	100.0
Provincial health facilities	78.9	15.7	5.4	100.0
District health facilities	78.6	11.2	10.2	100.0
CHCs	90.4	0.9	8.7	100.0
Private health facilities	92.7	2.0	5.3	100.0
Other	85.6	14.4	0.0	100.0
Total	84.0	9.0	7.0	100.0

Source: VWU (2012)

In general, health facilities have improved in infrastructure, facilities and human resources. Procedures are now much simpler than before, especially for those having health insurance. We are quite satisfied with their services. However, even at district hospitals, we sometimes have to wait for hours to get help.

(FGD, Ben Tre province)

5.5 Discussion and policy implications

Adapting to an ageing population means that the healthcare system in Vietnam has to be transformed to provide more geriatric services to OPs. There have been certain achievements in this transformation, but also various challenges which in turn require more concrete policy actions in order to protect the health rights of OPs and help them attain healthy ageing in the coming time.

First, in terms of services provided to OPs, although some services on mental healthcare for OPs have been in place for many years, especially at the community level, there have not yet been any policies/interventions for emerging diseases accounting for a large share of burden of disease among OPs (such as dementia). Also, there are no specific policies and programmes on reproductive healthcare for OPs, even though it was indicated in the National Plan of Action for Older People. Home-based care services, particularly palliative care, for OPs are increasingly important because a large number among them have difficulties or losses of mobility and/or vision, but the Law on Examination and Treatment does not provide a legal basis for setting up home-based healthcare services. Only service providers registered as family doctor clinics are allowed to provide curative care services at home, but their numbers are extremely limited.

Second, in terms of human resources for geriatric services, to date there are no standards for geriatric medicine specialisation to help in determining the scope of practice of geriatric specialists. In addition, there is yet to be any geriatric competency standards for general doctors, family doctors, internal medicine physicians and geriatric physicians. In addition, there are no provisions on continuing medical education to improve the general knowledge of health workers on the special needs of older patients (such as drug interactions, psychology of OPs in general and sick older people, in particular, counselling on diet and self-management of diseases).

Third, although SHI has played a more significant role in protecting OPs in financing for healthcare services, there is still a large financial burden for some groups of OPs, especially those living in rural areas where adequate health services are limited. Such a burden is heavier when OPs receive treatment at health facilities with higher technical services, especially those in the provincial and central levels, because there is a lack of financial mechanisms to encourage OPs to use services at the commune level. Older people want to use hospital services in order to receive reimbursements for the costs of medical examination and treatment medications for non-communicable diseases (NCD) or for rehabilitation services from SHI. Decisions to use hospital services drives them to higher levels of care, rather than accessing services provided at the commune level.

In conclusion, the need for healthcare services among OPs at present is quite substantial, primarily at the grassroots level, with a focus on preventive care and health promotion, screening for early detection and management of disease, rehabilitation for NCDs and impaired functional capacities. However, currently the scale of organisation of the geriatrics care network is extremely modest, and trained human resources are very limited. At the same time, the organisation and operational mechanism of the health system lacks inter-linkages which adversely affects capacity to provide comprehensive and continuous care for OPs. The grassroots-level and preventive medicine system have yet to be adequately standardised to meet the growing healthcare needs of OPs. Moreover, many health workers are yet to receive training to boost their knowledge and skills in providing healthcare for OPs. Capacity to provide preventive medicine services is also inadequate. Besides, periodic health check-ups, screening for early detection and management of disease in order to control NCDs in general is quite limited. Some health services specific to OPs, like rehabilitation in the community, palliative care, end-of-life care and home health services are yet to receive adequate attention. Even though there are many policies to support healthcare for OPs, the financial burden for families remains high. Therefore, in addition to organising provisions of healthcare services for OPs, health financial protection measures should aim at increasing ability to access and use healthcare services and, in turn, to reduce the risk of catastrophic spending among Vietnamese households.

References

Giang, T.L. and D.T. Bui (2013) "Access of Older People to Health Insurance and Healthcare Services in Vietnam: Current State and Policy Options". *Asia Pacific Population Journal*, 28(2): 69–89.

Giang, T.L., Pham, T.H.T. and L.T. Pham (2016, September) "Bao hiem y te trong cham soc suc khoe nguoi cao tuoi o Vietnam" (Social Health Insurance in Health Care for Older People in Vietnam). *Journal of Economics & Development*, 231(II): 38–48.

GSO (General Statistics Office, Vietnam) (various years) *Statistical Yearbook*. Hanoi: GSO.

———. (2011) *Population Projections 2009–2049: Key Results*. Hanoi: GSO.

Nguyen, V. C (2010) "Mapping the Reform Process in the Public Delivery of Health Services in Viet Nam". A background paper for Vietnam Human Development Report (VHDR) 2011. Hanoi: VASS-UNDP

Nguyen, V.C. and T.L. Giang (2012) *Access to Social Protection Services of the Most Vulnerable Groups of People in Viet Nam: A Sketch From Viet Nam Household Living Standards Surveys*. Hanoi: UNFPA.

Pham, T. and T.K.H. Do (2009) *Overview on Policies for Elderly Care to Adapt With Age Structure Changes of Population in Vietnam*. Hanoi: UNFPA.

UNFPA (United Nations Population Fund) (2011) *The Aging Population in Vietnam: Current Status, Prognosis, and Possible Policy Responses*. Hanoi: UNFPA.

VWU (Vietnam Women Union) (2012) *Vietnam Aging Survey: Key Findings*. Hanoi: Women's Publishing House.

6 Myanmar

Hein Thet Ssoe, S. Irudaya Rajan and Sreerupa

6.1 Introduction

World Health Organization (WHO) member countries endorsed a resolution to provide universal health coverage as early as in 2005. But very few low-income countries have come close to achieving the objective (Jacobs, Ir, Bigdeli, Annear and Van Damme 2012). Primarily, there have been numerous supply- and demand-side challenges and barriers that hamper access to needed health services. Significantly, the last time WHO ranked 191 countries across the globe based on overall health system performance, Myanmar ranked at the bottom of the list against its global counterparts (WHO 2000; Tandon, Murray, Lauer and Evans 2000). A recent study by WHO to review the health system of Myanmar revealed that over the years, Myanmar's health system has suffered from gaps in supply-side investments as well as demand-side challenges and health inequities (WHO 2014).

Decades of political unrest, armed conflicts, military rule, isolation and poor economic management have resulted in a weakened economy and poor public expenditure for basic services, including health services. Over the years, the public health system in Myanmar has remained severely under-resourced and neglected, with the vast majority of the burden of healthcare expenses being borne by the households (WHO 2014). Myanmar is one of the poorest countries in Asia and about one fourth of its population live below the poverty line (approximately 1,030 Kyats per adult, per day). Thus, one of the major challenges faced by Myanmar is providing healthcare in an equitable way to the poorest of the population without increasing their burden of expenditure (WHO 2014).

In low-income countries like Myanmar, healthcare and related expenditures have featured prominently as causes of impoverishment (Van Doorslaer et al. 2006). In this context, older persons (OPs) form a "vulnerable group" (Knodel 2014; Teerawichitchainan and Knodel 2015) of healthcare service users, and older women are particularly at risk of poor access to and utilisation of healthcare services (Sreerupa and Rajan 2010). Furthermore, confronted with the demographic and epidemiological transition, low-income countries such as Myanmar will face a massive public health challenge. While high-income countries have had a century to adjust to an ageing population as the proportion of older adults doubled from 7 percent to 14 percent, low-income countries like Myanmar is expected to make this shift in less than one-quarter of the time (Kinsella and He 2009). Similarly, a transition from communicable to non-communicable diseases (NCDs) will add a double burden of diseases on an already overstretched healthcare system. In this context, access to healthcare services becomes crucial to addressing the public health challenges posed by a fast-ageing population with a growing burden of diseases.

In a country with around 51 million people, slightly less than 5 million people are aged 60 years or above. Just about every tenth person in Myanmar is an older person, with the proportion of elderly at around 9 percent, according to the 2014 Myanmar census. It has been noted that in Myanmar, as in most other countries in Southeast Asia, not only have the numbers of persons in the old age cohorts been increasing but also their share of the total population (Knodel 2014). Within Myanmar, the proportion of elderly in the population is highest in Magway (10.8 percent) and lowest in Kayah (6 percent). Except Kachin and Kayah, all other states and regions fall into the United Nations-defined "ageing" category, meaning people 60 years old and above account for 7 percent or more of the total population. As in other countries, the proportion of elderly is highest among females and thus they enjoy a higher life expectancy. The life expectancy at birth over the years has shown remarkable improvement. During 1950–1955, it was just 36.8 years. It increased to 56.2 years during 2000–2005 and is expected to increase by 15.8 years by 2050. The size of the male–female gap in life expectancy is also increasing over the years.

Over a period of these 100 years, the growth rate of the elderly population in Myanmar has nearly always been higher than the total population growth rate, with the difference in growth rate widening from 2010 onwards. The proportion of elderly to the total population has increased over the years from 5.6 percent in 1950 to 7.1 percent in 2000. By 2050, the elderly proportion is expected to more than double and reach 20.2 percent of the total population according to census estimates.

6.2   Health status of older people

The health status of Myanmar's older persons (OPs) has been mapped out by utilising different health parameters such as self-rated health status, self-reported systems, prevalence of NCDs, disability and functional limitations and risk behaviours. In order to assess the older people's needs for healthcare, these health parameters are analysed by age, gender and area of residence.

6.2.1   Self-rated health status

Although the self-assessed current health status is a subjective measure associated with the feeling of well-being and quality of life, it has been found to be a reliable predictor of future functional status and even mortality (Idler and Benyamini 1997; Idler and Kasl 1995), thereby providing an empirical support

Table 6.1 Self-rated health status by age, gender and area of residence

Self-rated health	Total	Age			Gender		Area of residence	
		60–69	*70–79*	*80+*	*Male*	*Female*	*Urban*	*Rural*
Excellent/Good	37.9	40.1	38.2	28.5	43.0	34.0	38.3	37.7
Fair	29.0	30.1	27.1	27.8	27.3	30.3	27.7	29.7
Poor/Very poor	33.1	29.8	34.7	43.7	29.8	35.6	34	32.6

Source: Own calculations from the survey

for the use of this parameter as one of the measures of overall health. Data from Myanmar was found that on average, every third older person reported either "poor" or "very poor" health status, while slightly more reported their health to be "good" or "excellent". Across age groups, negative self-assessment of health increases at higher age groups and positive self-assessment correspondingly decreases. More than 40 percent of those 80 years and above reported "poor" to "very poor" health in comparison to only about 30 percent among those 60 to 70 years old. These relations are also inverted for reports of "good" to "excellent" health. Comparing men and women, there were 5 percent more women than men who reported to be in "poor" or "very poor" health, and nearly 10 percent more men than women who reported to be in "good" or "excellent" health. In general, men reported better health status than women. There was not much difference in self-perception of health when comparing urban and rural residents.

6.2.2   Self-reported symptoms

In a population with lower levels of awareness and recognition of ailments and diseases, self-reporting of specific symptoms related to illnesses would be a useful indicator of poor health and undiagnosed diseases. In the 2016 "Survey of access to health-care among older people in Myanmar", respondents were enquired whether they had experienced any of the 18 particular symptoms during the past month.

The single most common symptom reported was joint pain, of which 60 percent of OPs experienced. The other two most common symptoms were weakness and dizziness reported by 42 and 39 percent of the respondents, respectively. Across the different symptoms enquired, those 80 years and above and women were more likely to report symptoms in comparison with those 60 to 70 years old and men. No clear-cut pattern of difference was found between rural and urban populations. The results from the 2016 survey were also found to be consistent with trends found in the report, The Situation of Older Persons in Myanmar: Results From the 2012 Survey of Older Persons (Rev. 2014) (Knodel 2014), although there was a slightly higher reporting of symptoms in general in the latter.

6.2.3   Non-communicable diseases

Once known as "diseases of affluence", the NCDs are no longer a problem only in the wealthy countries (WHO 2011a). In fact, the years of life lost to NCDs among people of aged 60 and above in low- and middle-income countries are much greater than for people in high-income countries (Scommegna 2012). According to the World Health Organization, the NCDs constitute approximately 40 percent of all deaths in Myanmar (WHO 2011b).

One of the most common NCDs is hypertension, and more than one-third of the elderly population in Myanmar has been diagnosed with high blood pressure in accordance with WHO's criteria. The other common NCDs are cardiovascular diseases, cataracts, stroke and arthritis. A high prevalence of NCDs increases the need for healthcare among OPs. A fragile national healthcare system that has focused more on tackling infectious diseases, however, would be severely tested by the contracted nature of NCDs, which may lead to an increasing healthcare burden on the national budget.

6.2.4   Disability and functional limitations

Mobility limitations are often the early sign of subsequent functional decline among OPs. The respondents of the survey were asked whether or not they had difficulty moving around by themselves. Four percent of a sample of 1000 respondents reported that they could not move at all. Differences in accordance with age, gender and area of residence were obvious from the responses. Albeit there is not much variation between men and women in the category of people who cannot move at all, more older women than men reported that they had difficulties with mobility. The results revealed that the inability to move around increases proportionately with age, i.e. more than 10 percent in the oldest category reported that they were unable to move around. Apropos of the area of residence, survey findings show that urban residents suffer more than their rural counterparts.

Pertaining to the responses of whether or not they had experienced bodily aches and pains, 7 percent expressed they did. More than 2 percent complained that they could not move anything at all because of bodily aches and pains. The situation of women had been found to be much poorer than that of men. In regards to the different age cohorts, the elderly experienced more difficulties than other age groups in that they were more likely to experience constant aches and pains. Concerning urban–rural differences, the proportion of respondents who experienced severe difficulty is larger in the urban areas than in the rural areas.

In the case of sense organs, particularly vision and hearing, nearly 2 percent of the respondents are legally blind and almost 12 percent could see, only with much difficulty. There is a wide variation between men and women, with more females in the category of those who could see but with great difficulty compared with males. Those 80 years old and above are the main sufferers, and more urban residents expressed difficulties with their vision than rural residents.

Regarding respondents' abilities to hear what is said in a conversation with others, nearly 2 percent were found not to be able to hear at all. There are more women than men in the category of those who could not hear but only with a lot of difficulty. Hearing problems increased with age and more than 7 percent among the oldest age group could not hear at all. There is not much difference between urban and rural residents with respect to declining degree of hearing ability.

6.2.5 Risk behaviours

Questions related to the use of tobacco, alcohol and betel were asked in the survey. Around one-third of the respondents admitted using betel and tobacco products. In general, alcohol consumption among OPs was significantly less than tobacco and betel use. The use of all three substances was higher among men than women. Consumption of both alcohol and betel was found to be lower in the older age groups, whereas consumption of tobacco products still remained high even among the oldest age group. The use of tobacco products and alcohol was found to be higher among rural residents, and the intake of betel was higher among urban residents.

6.3 Healthcare systems and policies focusing on older people

Compared with other countries in Southeast Asia and Western Pacific regions, the expenditure for health in Myanmar is the lowest (WHO 2014). It averaged about 2 percent of GDP in 2000–2011. In 2011, the government's share in the health sector constituted merely 13 percent; the rest of the expenditure burden has to be borne through out-of-pocket (OOP) household expenses, which translate into 79 percent of the total expenditure (WHO 2014). The remaining – around 7 percent – is contributed by national and international donors. Moreover, the previous government which assumed power in 2011 demonstrated commitment to the undertaking, and the health spending by the state quadrupled in 2012–2013 (WHO 2014).

The Myanmar healthcare system currently encounters a range of problems related to the availability and distribution of supply-side factors such as human resources, physical infrastructure, service delivery and financial resources. In addition, the healthcare system is characterised by weaknesses in supportive supervision, referral, the health management information system, public finance management, oversight, leadership and accountability.

6.3.1 Human resources for health

The Myanmar Health Workforce Strategic Plan for the period 2012–2017 described the current human resources obstacles, which include shortages of human resources, inappropriate balance and mix of skills, inequitable distribution of manpower and difficulties in maintaining rural retention. As of November 2016, there were 1.33 healthcare workers (i.e. doctors, nurses and midwives) per 1,000 people (MoHS 2014), well below the WHO minimum recommended threshold of 2.3. In terms of distribution, health workers were largely concentrated in urban areas such as Yangon, Mandalay and NayPyiTaw. A mechanism for the accreditation of educational programmes and institutions by external bodies has been recently developed. The Professional Councils are expected to design an accreditation system in line with international standards. Discussions have been already initiated with the Myanmar Medical Council (MMC) and the Myanmar Nurse and Midwife Council (MNMC). In fact, the MNMC has recently drafted accreditation guidelines for training institutions and has planned to begin implementing accreditation activities upon official approval.

Pre-service training of all healthcare professionals in Myanmar is the responsibility of the Department of Human Resources for Health (HRH). As of June 2016, there were 12,230 medical students and 7,572 nursing and midwifery students out of the overall total of 29,528 students in health-related studies (MoHS 2014). These numbers demonstrate a sharp increase from previous years, further exacerbating the inequality in comparison to the training of Basic Health Staff (BHS), even if the population served by BHS in rural areas is much larger than that served by doctors and nurses.

The lack of clear recruitment and deployment policies do not help the current scenario. In addition, there is limited clarity about the roles and responsibilities of disparate healthcare professionals at all levels of the system. This explains at least partially why midwives are overburdened. Even though they are extensively trained to perform midwifery matters, additional tasks not related to midwifery are commonly assigned to them.

Deployment and in-service training are the joint responsibility of the Department of Public Health and Department of Medical Services. Currently, the in-service trainings are disproportionately project-orientated and as a consequence hindering continuous professional development. Given the convenient dependency on projects, the sustainability of these and ad hoc in-service training becomes doubtful.

6.3.2   *Physical infrastructure*

Having merely human resources for health is not enough. There needs to be a balanced distribution of infrastructure such as buildings and equipment. Currently, there is no clear-cut nationwide infrastructure investment plan. There is often a mismatch between health administrative maps and catchment areas of health facilities, leading to difficulties in estimating the catchment population.

The design of health facilities can vary depending on the source of funding. This suggests that not all health facilities have essential amenities such as clean water, sanitation, reliable electric supply, warehousing facilities, staff accommodation, and transport and communication provisions.

Furthermore, restrictions imposed by financial rules and regulations and the lack of operational budget for maintenance have led to the unnecessary delays in the tendering process. Efforts to allow budgetary flexibility for maintenance purposes are still ongoing. Transportation between health facilities is yet another impediment, increasing the barriers to accessing health services.

6.3.3 *Service delivery*

Service delivery in Myanmar relies on a mix of healthcare providers from the following sectors: public (state), private for-profit, private non-profit, and Ethnic Health Organisations (EHOs). Ministry of Health and Sports (MoHS) has been leading technical activities since 2014 to define the Essential Package of Health Services (EPHS). The plan is to have a Basic EPHS by 2020, an intermediate EPHS by 2025 and a comprehensive EPHS by 2030.

The current public health services provision focuses on tertiary care, which means station hospitals and below have received less over the past few decades. This kind of underinvestment has caused various shortcomings in service availability, readiness, standards and coverage. In addition, there is limited public-sector service delivery in both conflict-affected and post-conflict-affected areas.

It has been recognised that the public sector alone is not able to reach the entire population with the basic EPHS itself. The public sector's resources vary in terms of their level of readiness, while other sectors such as private for-profit providers, NGOs and EHOs are also involved in service delivery. However, government oversight and engagement are limited. Among all types of service providers, quality of care has the greatest variations.

EHOs have long been providing essential services and interventions to populations in conflict-affected areas where public sector services could not reach. Despite recent promising initiatives, standardisation of these services among different EHOs and between EHOs themselves and the public sector faces various political as well as technical challenges. The different kinds of healthcare workers employed by EHOs are currently trained through parallel systems with limited or no recognition from MoHS. Since service provisions by EHOs rely heavily on donors' support, their sustainability is often at risk. Existing procurement and supply chain arrangements are highly fragmented along vertical programmes and funding sources. This fragmentation complicates coordination and creates inefficiencies, duplication and wastages. Weak policies and regulations, their limited enforcements and lack of clarity in existing guidelines pose further challenges. Underinvestment in MoHS procurement and the supply chain management system has translated into limited management capacity, and inadequate infrastructure and technology. The existing paper-based management information system deters the timely aggregation of data and limits its use.

Budget execution, or drawing rights, is decentralised only to Township Medical Officers. There is no fund flow to health facilities below the township level. Reallocation of funds between budget lines during the fiscal year is almost impossible for implementers. That, combined with the fact that the budget does not match the needs and that unused funds cannot be transferred to the next year, results in low levels of expenditure. Current financial regulations are no longer suitable for the purpose, particularly those regarding advances, travel allowances, phone bills, petrol/gas and other petty operational expenses. Financial management capacity is low within MoHS at all levels, with an inadequate number of financial management professionals.

Financial reporting focuses on inputs and on fulfilling audit requirements, rather than on outputs and achievements. The system is still fully paper-based and administratively heavy. There is also very little evidence that the information from financial reports is being used in decision-making.

6.3.4   *Financial resources*

Myanmar currently allocates 3.65 percent of its total government budget on health, which is extremely low, by global and regional standards according to the Myanmar Ministry of Planning and Finance. Some reprioritisation processes towards social sectors in general, and the health sector in particular, have already taken place in recent years. The nine-fold increase in absolute amount, i.e. from US$94 million in 2010–2011 to US$850 million in 2016–2017 was mainly used to finance the delivery of healthcare and expansion of service coverage with a focus-free medical care in hospital settings.

Funding from other sources, including from development partners (DPs), is largely channelled through parallel systems. In addition to making oversight and coordination difficult, this results in inefficiencies and does not contribute to strengthening the government institutional capacity.

6.4   Assessing health security for older people

6.4.1   *Assessment methods*

This study is from the perspective of OPs as recipients or targets of healthcare services and uses a mixed method research design. The methodology includes a quantitative component employing a household survey and a qualitative component using post-survey focus group discussions among older persons in target communities. The sample of communities/households has been taken from one township in each of five geographic areas of the country: hilly, delta, dry zone, plain/coastal and metropolitan.

Household survey

SAMPLING METHOD

The sample was distributed between five townships using the 80:20 rural-to-urban ratio. This method was used to estimate the sample for all regions except Yangon, which is a metropolitan area. In Yangon, the study was conducted in wards instead of villages. The Probability Proportionate to Size (PPS) method was used to determine the number of wards or villages within townships, to ensure that the sampling was systematic and produced estimates with minimum bias. The sample of wards and villages was selected based on the population of OPs per township. In the study, the total sample was 1000 OPs. Furthermore, a sample of 200 respondents were selected from each of the five townships consisting of both wards and villages.

HOUSEHOLD SELECTION

Households were selected by conducting a random walk in the Primary Sampling Unit (PSU), following the Right-Hand Rule. After every interview attempt, whether successful or not, the enumerator skipped to another household within a specified interval. Eligible respondents – those aged 60 years and above – were interviewed from sampled households. As recommended by the researcher, in cases of more than one eligible respondent in the sampled household, the data collection agency interviewed all the eligible respondents until the target sample of 20 OPs was reached per PSU.

Focus group discussions

Semi-structured focus group discussions (FGDs) were conducted among respondents with sufficient numbers of persons starting from the cohort 60 years and older. These FGDs aimed at capturing older persons' experiences and perceptions on seeking healthcare while allowing them to raise the issues and concerns that are most important to them. For each of the five geographical regions, two to four FGDs were conducted. Each FGD consisted of 10 to 15 respondents. Each FGD lasted for no more than two hours. Oral consent was obtained from the respondents at the beginning of each FGD. FGDs were translated into English and the transcripts were thematically analysed.

6.4.2 Key findings

Accessibility

GEOGRAPHIC ACCESSIBILITY OF OUTPATIENT HEALTHCARE (SUPPLY SIDE)

The time required to get to a healthcare facility may be considered a barrier for accessing healthcare. About 88 percent of the elderly people accessing local drug stores and 76 percent of those utilising sub-rural health centres (SRHCs) and rural health centres (RHCs) took less than 30 minutes to get to the healthcare provider of their choice. On the other hand, merely 45 percent of the respondents seeking outpatient care at a township or district hospital could reach the facility in less than 30 minutes, and some 30 percent even needed more than an hour. Taken as a whole, the local drug stores and the primary healthcare centres such as SRHCs and RHCs are apparently more closely situated and therefore more promptly accessible, while the government healthcare centres appear to be the farthest away and thus took the longest time to access (Table 6.2).

Table 6.2 Time taken to reach the various outpatient healthcare facilities (percent distribution)

	Total	Drug stores	Sub-RHCs and RHCs	Private doctors	Private clinics and hospitals	Government hospitals
Below 30 min.	64.1	88.2	75.7	67.0	56.4	44.9
30 to 60 min.	21.1	8.8	16.8	19.1	24.8	25.6
60 min. and more	14.8	2.9	7.5	13.9	18.8	29.5
Total	100	100	100	100	100	100

Source: Own calculations from the survey

Table 6.3 Means of transport to reach an outpatient healthcare facility, by type of healthcare provider (percent distribution)

Mode of Transport	Total	Drug stores	Sub-RHCs and RHCs	Private doctors	Private clinics and hospitals	Government hospitals
Private Vehicle	20.9	21.1	24.2	22.0	21.3	22.7
Public Transportation	10.6	10.5	0.0	13.0	18.7	12.0
Taxi	23.4	5.3	16.2	27.6	27.3	41.3
Walked	27.7	34.2	52.5	25.2	14.0	6.7
Bicycle/Trishaw	13.6	28.9	3.0	12.2	18.7	17.3

Source: Own calculations from the survey

GEOGRAPHIC ACCESSIBILITY OF OUTPATIENT HEALTHCARE (DEMAND SIDE)

Means of transportation   The respondents' means of transportation and the cost of transportation impact on the ease at which a patient is able to access healthcare services. The data from the study showed that ordinarily 21 percent of the respondents used private vehicles, without much appreciable differences across the diverse healthcare facilities. Furthermore, about 10 percent of the respondents use public transportation, with the exception of those who obtained treatment from the PHCs and private clinics and hospitals. Throughout the different healthcare facilities, there exists considerable variation in the utilisation of various modes of travel such as walking with assistance, if needed, bicycles, motorbikes, trishaws, small tractors and taxis (Table 6.3).

As the local drug stores and the primary healthcare centres (PHCs) tend to be quite close to the home, elderly people, on average, either walked or made use of bicycles, motorbikes, trishaws or small tractors to get to the centres; only 5 to 16 percent took taxis to access the services provided at PHCs. In contrast, only 24 percent of the OPs accessing outpatient care at the township and district hospitals reached the health facilities by walking or taking a bicycle, motorbike, trishaw or small tractor, and 41 percent used taxis, implying that government hospitals are less accessible than the local drug stores and PHCs. With regard to the private-sector healthcare facilities, it was found that there is a more even mix of private and public transport that was used, suggesting a more moderate level of accessibility.

Cost of transportation   Provided the transportation costs could be lowered the geographical accessibility aspect could obviously be much improved (Jacobs et al. 2012). The implication is that in a poverty-stricken country such as Myanmar, the cost of transportation could well be an important barrier to accessing the necessary healthcare services.

The study shows that the median cost of transportation is the lowest for accessing the local drug stores and PHCs i.e. 0 Kyat, with more than 50 percent of OPs either walking or riding bicycles or trishaws to access these centres. The median cost of transportation to the private centres is between MMK 500–1,000 in comparison to the median cost of travel to the government hospitals of 1,000 MMK (Table 6.4).

Apropos the demand and supply side of geographical barriers, it appears that the access barriers are the highest for government hospitals, followed by the private-sector-run facilities, while the local drug stores and PHCs seem to be the most geographically accessible. In the FGDs, respondents said that the small, local medicine shops, especially the nearby grocery stores that also sell basic medications and the SRHCs, particularly in the main village in the village tracts, are often the easiest and cheapest to access in terms of geographical accessibility, since such shops and SRHCs tend to be conveniently located. As for the private healthcare facilities such as clinics and hospitals, as they are usually located in or near the urban areas, they are also

Table 6.4 Cost of transport to reach an outpatient healthcare facility, by type of provider (percent distribution and median cost in Myanmar kyat)

Mode of Transport	Total	Drug stores	Sub-RHCs and RHCs	Private doctors	Private clinics and hospitals	Government hospitals
Less than 1000 kyat (percent)	57.8	85.3	76.4	51.3	41.6	38.5
1000 to 3000 kyat (percent)	24.8	14.7	11.8	29.6	38.9	26.9
3000 kyat or more (percent)	15.0	0.0	5.5	17.4	18.1	32.1
Median cost (in kyat)	0.0	0.0	0.0	500.0	1000.0	1000.0

Source: Own calculations from the survey

Table 6.5 Time required to reach the hospital or inpatient healthcare facility (percent distribution)

Time	Township and Station Hospitals	District and General Hospitals	Private hospitals	Total
Less than 30 minutes	28.6	17.0	4.3	18.8
30 to 60 minutes	31.7	17.0	30.4	24.3
60 to 120 minutes	27.0	31.9	26.1	28.4
120 minutes and more	12.7	34.1	39.2	28.5

Source: Own calculations from the survey

farther away and more expensive and less convenient to access. More often than not, the government clinics and hospitals happen to be the most expensive and farthest facilities to access.

GEOGRAPHIC ACCESSIBILITY OF INPATIENT HEALTHCARE (SUPPLY SIDE)

The time spent to get to a healthcare centre from the household could be regarded as an indicator of geographic barriers in accessing a healthcare centre (Table 6.5). Table shows that the closest hospitals are the station or the township hospitals. Approximately 60 percent of OPs were able to reach these facilities within an hour. In contrast, the district or the general hospitals and the private clinics or hospitals are among the farthest with more than 65 percent of OPs requiring over an hour to reach these facilities.

GEOGRAPHIC ACCESSIBILITY OF INPATIENT HEALTHCARE (DEMAND SIDE)

Cost of transport   The average cost of transportation to a station or a township hospital is proportionately lower at about MMK 4,000. In comparison, the cost of transportation to a private hospital is MMK 10,000 and to a district or general hospital is MMK 11,500. One-third of OPs accessing a station or a township hospital ran up transportation costs of less than MMK 2,000, while 22 percent incurred more than MMK 14,000. Only 9 percent of OPs seeking hospitalisation in private facilities incurred less than MMK 2,000 for transportation costs. 45 percent of OPs accessing the district or general hospitals spent more than MMK 14,000 for transportation (Table 6.6).

The massive cost of transportation to get to a district or general hospital presents a considerable geographic barrier that could constrain a sizeable number of poor rural people from accessing specialised care provided at these facilities. Overall, it could be said that these demand-side and supply-side parameters suggest the highest geographical barriers for OPs accessing district or general hospitals and private facilities. The station or township hospitals instead become the most geographically accessible inpatient healthcare services.

Table 6.6 Cost of transport to reach the inpatient healthcare facility, by type of healthcare provider (percent distribution and median cost)

Cost of Transport	Township and station hospitals	District and general hospitals	Private hospitals	Total
Less than 2,000 kyats (percent)	33.3	17	8.7	22.2
2,000 to 8,000 kyats (percent)	23.8	21.3	30.4	22.9
8,000 to 14,000 kyats (percent)	17.5	14.9	17.4	17.4
More than 14,000 kyats (percent)	22.2	44.7	39.1	34.7
Median cost (in kyat)	4,000	11,500	10,000	10,000

Source: Own calculations from the survey

Table 6.7 Total cost incurred for outpatient treatment, by type of healthcare provider (percent distribution and median cost)

Total Cost	Total	Drug stores	Sub-RHCs and RHCs	Private doctors	Private clinics and hospitals	Gov't hospitals
Less than 3,000 kyats (percent)	32.5	73.5	47.3	20.0	17.4	25.6
3,000 to 9,000 kyats (percent)	42.2	20.6	40.0	51.3	48.3	38.5
9,000 to 15,000 kyats (percent)	6.1	0.0	2.7	10.4	8.1	5.1
15,000 kyats and more (percent)	18.5	5.9	9.1	17.4	25.5	30.8
Median cost (in kyat)	4,000	2,000	3,000	5,000	6,000	5,000

Source: Own calculations from the survey

Affordability

AFFORDABILITY OF OUTPATIENT HEALTHCARE (SUPPLY SIDE)

The cost of service delivery is a considerable supply-side barrier. The usual total cost of outpatient care across the spectra of healthcare providers is shown in Table 6.7. The lowest average cost of outpatient care was found to be provided by drugstores (MMK 2,000), followed by SRHCs and RHCs (MMK 3,000), then private doctors and government hospitals (MMK 5,000). Private clinics and hospitals were the least affordable, with the total cost of outpatient care averaging around MMK 6,000. Nearly three-quarters of OPs visiting drugstores and half of the OPs visiting SRHCs and RHCs accessed these services for less than MMK 3,000 compared with about one-quarter of OPs visiting other facilities. Private clinics and hospitals, followed by private doctors and government hospitals, are the most expensive sources of outpatient care, while the least expensive ones are the drugstores and primary healthcare centres.

Another potential supply-side barrier to the outpatient healthcare is the presence of a public–private dual practice, which exposes the elderly patients to public health workers' private practice, increasing the chances of spiralling treatment costs, not to mention the potential implementation of double standards and occurrence of conflicts of interest.

From the fieldwork, we met one elderly lady whose experience is a typical case of a patient seeking treatment from a specialist doctor at a private hospital. The elderly lady saw a specialist doctor at a private hospital and at each visit she had to buy the medicines prescribed by the specialist which were quite expensive. After about ten visits, she could no longer afford the cost of medicines charged by the hospital pharmacy and inquired about the medicines at another pharmacy outside the hospital. Only then did she find out that the medicines at the second pharmacy cost only half the price. By that time, however, she had needed to sell some of her land to defray the cost of medical care.

AFFORDABILITY OF OUTPATIENT HEALTHCARE (DEMAND SIDE)

There is also the cost of outpatient care as a percentage of household expenditure. The total cost of the respondents most recently received outpatient care as a percentage of the household total monthly expenditure has been calculated to assess the demand-side cost barriers to outpatient care. Overall, the median total cost of the most recent outpatient care was about 3 percent of the household median monthly expenditure. The median total cost of the outpatient care accounted for around 3 percent of rural households' median monthly expenditure, and 4 percent of the poorest households' (in the "lower" category of the Wealth Index) median monthly expenditure. In contrast, the median total cost of the most recent outpatient care was 2 percent of both the urban households' and the richest households' (upper end of the Wealth Index) median monthly expenditure.

The cost of outpatient care in relation to average monthly expenditure is nearly double for the poorest households (4 percent) as compared to the richest households (2 percent). This highlights the concern of the burden of outpatient care expenses on the poorer households, especially when these households have been found to be accessing the cheaper sources of outpatient care (Table 6.8). Other important demand-side barriers identified in the literature are the general lack of economic resources and, more specifically, the low availability of liquid cash when the patient is seeking medical care (Khun and Manderson 2007).

AFFORDABILITY OF INPATIENT HEALTHCARE (SUPPLY SIDE)

The average total cost of hospitalisation was found to be lowest for station or township hospitals (MMK 70,000), followed by the district and general hospitals (MMK 110,000). Private hospitals were the least affordable, with

Table 6.8 Healthcare provider or facility visited for outpatient healthcare in the preceding 12 months, by area of residence and relative wealth (percent distribution)

Type of Healthcare Provider or Facility	Total	Area of residence		Wealth Index			
		Urban	Rural	Lower	Lower-middle	Middle	Upper
Drug stores	6.6	5.9	7.1	3.0	4.7	9.1	8.8
Sub-RHC and RHCs	17.3	2.5	27.7	40.6	16.3	13.7	4.8
Private doctors	21.5	25.3	18.8	12.9	19.2	25.1	26.4
Private clinic and hospitals	26.2	45.6	12.5	18.8	25.0	26.3	33.6
Government hospitals	13.1	11.4	14.3	8.9	15.7	14.3	11.2

Source: Own calculations from the survey

Table 6.9 Total cost to access inpatient healthcare services during the most recent hospital stay, by type of healthcare provider (percent distribution and median cost)

Total Cost	Township and station hospitals	District and general hospitals	Private hospitals	Total
Less than 50,000 kyats (percent)	33.3	21.2	0.0	23.6
50,000 to 150,000 kyats (percent)	34.9	38.3	30.4	36.1
150,000 to 250,000 kyats (percent)	14.3	12.8	17.4	13.9
250,000 kyats and above (percent)	17.5	27.7	52.2	26.4
Median cost (in kyat)	70,000	110,000	300,000	107,000

Source: Own calculations from the survey

the average total cost of hospitalisation at around MMK 300,000, which was three times more than the cost at the government hospitals. One-third of OPs hospitalised in station or township hospitals could access the services for less than MMK 50,000. In contrast, only one-fifth of OPs hospitalised in district or general hospitals, and none of those hospitalised in private hospitals could access the services for less than MMK 50,000. On the other hand, more than half the persons hospitalised in private hospitals cost more than MMK 250,000, in comparison to only 17 percent of those hospitalised in station or township hospitals. The total cost of hospitalisation throughout the different facilities shows that private hospitals were the least affordable, followed by district or general hospitals, and then station and township hospitals (Table 6.9).

AFFORDABILITY OF INPATIENT HEALTHCARE (DEMAND SIDE)

The total cost of hospitalisation as a percentage of a household's total monthly expenditure was calculated to access the demand-side barriers to hospitalisation. On average, the median total cost of a hospitalisation occurrence constituted more than 70 percent of the household's median monthly expenditure. It was found that the median total cost of the most recent hospitalisation accounted for more than 95 percent of the rural household's and 90 percent of the poorest households' median monthly expenditures, respectively. In comparison, the cost of the most recent hospitalisation constituted only about 50 percent of household median monthly expenditure for both the urban and the richest households. The average cost burden for hospitalisation in relation to average monthly expenditure is nearly double for rural and the poorest households, as compared to urban and the richest households. As mentioned in the discussion of outpatient healthcare, other important demand-side barriers include a general lack of economic resources i.e. poverty, particularly availability of liquid cash at the time the OP is seeking care (Khun and Manderson 2007).

Availability

A myriad of factors can affect whether adequate healthcare can be made available or not; however, often in the poorer countries, the root cause of supply-side barriers happens to be the sizeable gap existing between the actual spending on healthcare and the required spending to provide sufficient essential healthcare services (O'Donnell 2007; WHO 2001). The lack of adequate funding for the healthcare system emerges at the ground level in various forms: unqualified or underqualified health workers of different grades, insufficient number of health workers, frequent staff absenteeism, often late opening hours and early closing hours, unusual long waiting times and lists, lack of motivation among staff, paucity of availability of essential drugs and other ancillary paraphernalia. For instance in 2010–11, the ratio of doctors, nurses and midwives per 1,000 population was only 1.49, well below the global standard of 2.28 health workers per 1,000 population (WHO 2014). The long waiting times for services attest to the fact that staff and equipment are not equitably distributed according to needs (Jacobs et al. 2012). In addition, when the poorly paid public healthcare givers need to set up private practices or private–public dual practices, the availability of health staff at public facilities becomes a significant problem. Thus, the availability of adequate, timely, quality care made available to the population, specifically OPs, has been compromised by the burdens of staff absenteeism, limited opening hours, long waiting times and so on.

In order to determine the supply-side barriers to healthcare availability, a set of questions were asked of OPs, principally to assess their perceptions concerning "care and attention", "medical treatment", "availability of medicines", "waiting time" and "cleanliness" of their healthcare facilities. Respondents were then asked to rate how satisfied they were with the healthcare services they obtained on a five-point scale from "very satisfied" to "very dissatisfied". On the whole, only an extremely small number of OPs rated themselves to be "dissatisfied" or "very dissatisfied" with the healthcare they had received, which may be linked to cultural factors. This may indicate a reluctance to express dissatisfaction or low expectations on their part of services or both.

Subsequently, more respondents seemed to be rather willing to choose "indifference" about the quality of healthcare, exhorting one to combine the "neither satisfied nor dissatisfied" category with the "dissatisfied" and "very dissatisfied" categories, and use this as a substitute for some degree of inadequacy in satisfaction with the healthcare services.

Analysing OPs' perception of the care and attention they received, the quality of medical treatment, availability of medicines, waiting times and cleanliness of the facility throughout different healthcare facilities manifests the following, as captured in Figures 6.1–6.5. The highest percentage of respondents were "very satisfied" with the healthcare services provided by the private clinics and hospitals, followed by the private doctors, drugstores and lastly by RHCs, SRHCs and government hospitals, which comprised station and township hospitals and district and general hospitals. Furthermore, considering the percentage of OPs who said that they were "satisfied" with numerous aspects of healthcare availability, it becomes apparent that in general, respondents rate private facilities higher in comparison with the government-run PHCs like SRHCs and RHCs, and government hospitals, with respect to the care and attention they received, the quality of medical treatment and the availability of medicines.

One singular exception to the pattern is the measure of waiting time as shown in Figure 6.4. A higher proportion of the elderly people reported that overall

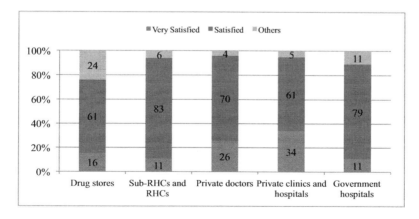

Figure 6.1 Perceptions of the care and attention received from the healthcare provider or facility during the most recent outpatient visit (percent distribution)

Source: Own calculations from the survey

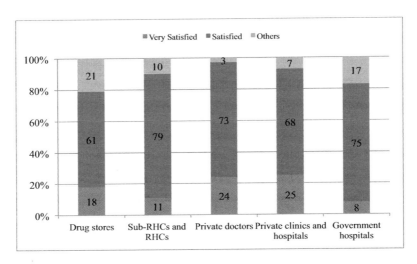

Figure 6.2 Perceptions of the medical treatment received from the healthcare provider or facility during the most recent outpatient visit (percent distribution)

Source: Own calculations from the survey

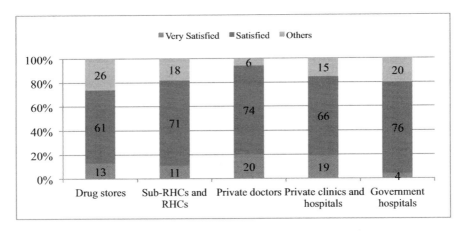

Figure 6.3 Perceptions of the availability of medicines at the healthcare provider or facility during the most recent outpatient visit (percent distribution)

Source: Own calculations from the survey

waiting time at the RHCs was better than at the private facilities, which might be explained by the structure of supply and demand. In addition, across the various modes of availability, the local drugstores had the highest percentage of OPs reporting either indifference or dissatisfaction, except with regard to waiting time. Somewhat paradoxically, the local drugstores were also among

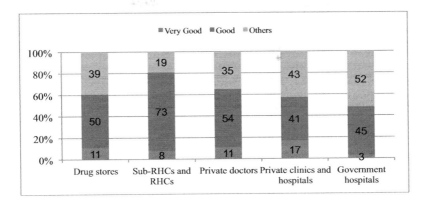

Figure 6.4 Perceptions of the waiting time for treatment at the healthcare provider or facility during the most recent outpatient visit (percent distribution)

Source: Own calculations from the survey

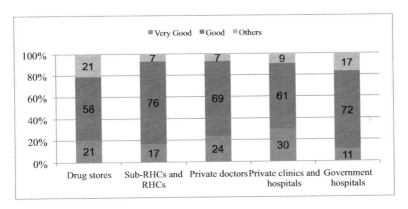

Figure 6.5 Perceptions of the cleanliness of the facility during the most recent outpatient visit (percent distribution)

Source: Own calculations from the survey

the top three outpatient care providers for which the highest percentage of OPs reported to be "very satisfied", behind the private facilities and ahead of government facilities. That there was a high proportion of both high and poor ratings on the range of modes of availability among local drugstores is fairly interesting. It may reflect a great deal of diversity within this category of providers, ranging from small neighbourhood drugstores to the big pharmacies, as well as the presence or absence of regulation, standardisation, supervision and training.

FGDs showed a range of OPs' perceptions about the availability of outpatient services at the various sources:

> *Concerning private facilities.* "If we go to the private clinic, on-duty medical staff is always present. The staff treats us attentively. There is neither a waiting list nor any need to come back later".
>
> *Concerning the SRHCs and RHCs.* "There is only one health worker for nearly 1,000 households". "Since the doctors are out of our reach we have to depend mainly on other health workers whether we like it or not . . . we need more qualified staff at the RHC". "There are frequent shortages of medicines at the RHC".
>
> *Concerning government hospitals.* "All the best doctors are in the government hospitals, but they do not have time and are always busy. These doctors spend some time at the government hospital and then work as consultants in private hospitals or work in their private clinics".

Some OPs in the urban areas were found to access charity-based clinics. During an FGD, an OP noted the barriers to accessing free outpatient care at these clinics:

> There is a charity medical care open to everyone, established by a well-known Buddhist monk. But the problem is the clinic only opens on Tuesdays and Fridays from 12 to 4 pm. As a result, the waiting time to recieve medical help is extremely long, which is not appropriate for elderly people.

AVAILABILITY OF INPATIENT HEALTHCARE (SUPPLY SIDE)

The supply-side barriers apropos of availability include the motivation of staff, the qualifications of staff, staff absenteeism, opening hours, wait lists and time and the availability of medications and other consumables (Jacobs et al. 2012). In order to determine the supply-side barriers concerned with the inpatient health availability, a set of questionnaires about OP's perceptions related to "care and attention", "medical treatment", "availability of medicines", "waiting times" and "cleanliness" at the healthcare facilities were utilised. The respondents were instructed to rate how satisfied they were with the healthcare services they obtained on a five-point scale of "very satisfied", "satisfied", "neither satisfied nor dissatisfied", "dissatisfied" and "very dissatisfied". As in the previous analysis of availability and acceptability of outpatient healthcare, an extremely low number of OPs responded by either stating "dissatisfied" or "very dissatisfied", prompting the surveyors once again to combine the "neither satisfied nor dissatisfied" rating with the poor rating and then using the combined score as a substitute for the rating "some extent of discontent".

On respondent perceptions of care and attention, medical treatment and the availability of medications received at the different healthcare facilities, the results showed that the highest percentage of OPs were "very satisfied" with the healthcare services received at the district or general hospitals and at private hospitals (Figures 6.6–6.8). A slightly higher percentage of OPs found the

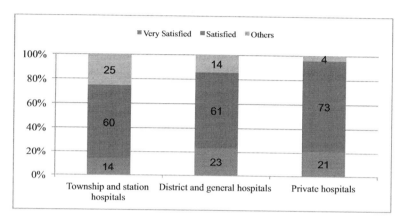

Figure 6.6 Perceptions of the care and attention received from the healthcare provider or facility during the most recent hospitalisation (percent distribution)
Source: Own calculations from the survey

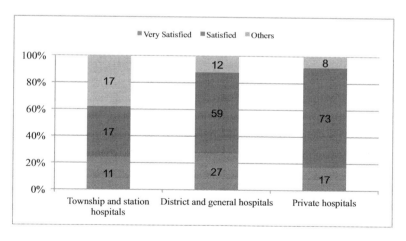

Figure 6.7 Perceptions of the medical treatment received from the healthcare provider or facility during the most recent hospitalisation (percent distribution)
Source: Own calculations from the survey

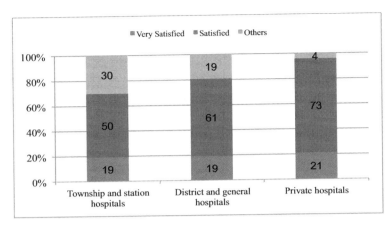

Figure 6.8 Perceptions of the availability of medicines at the healthcare facility during the most recent hospitalisation (percent distribution)

Source: Own calculations from the survey

medical treatment and the attention provided in the district or general hospitals to be "very satisfied", in comparison with other options. Upon combining "satisfied" and "very satisfied", however, it becomes apparent that more respondents preferred private facilities. In terms of the availability of medications, generally, the station or township hospitals received the lowest ratings on the above features. As a rule, ratings of the waiting time at the different types of hospitals followed a similar pattern, with more than a quarter of OPs reporting "moderate" to "very poor" (Figure 6.9). Concerning the cleanliness of the different health facilities, all OPs who had been hospitalised in the private facilities reported "good" or "very good", in contrast to the relatively poor ratings for cleanliness for both types of government-run facilities (Figure 6.10). Overall, the private facilities had been rated more favourably on the different measures of availability.

FGDs showed OP's dissatisfaction with the government-run general hospitals:

"There are about five private clinics in our area. But for the acute and serious cases, we must rely only on the general hospital. We do go to the private clinics sometimes not just because we have plenty of money but because they provide all the necessary medicines and supplies. Whereas in the general hospitals, they ask us to search and buy these [ourselves] which is very difficult."

"To be fair, nowadays, the general hospitals are getting better even though slowly. A lot of medicinal drugs and supplies are now available there. We only need to look for and buy some special medications or supplies."

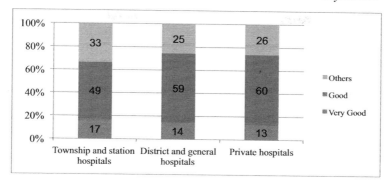

Figure 6.9 Perceptions of the waiting time for treatment at the healthcare provider or facility during the most recent hospitalisation (percent distribution)
Source: Own calculations from the survey

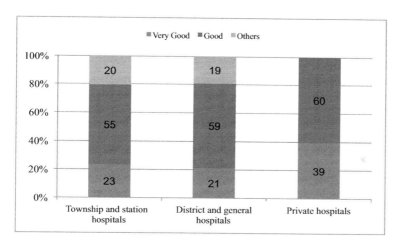

Figure 6.10 Perceptions of the cleanliness of the healthcare facility during the most recent hospitalisation (percent distribution)
Source: Own calculations from the survey

"One problem with the general hospitals is the awful smell which may be because of poor sanitation."

"All government hospitals have the waiting list system. That means when you get some symptoms you can't see the doctor straightaway. You have to book first before you can see him or her the next day. All government appointed doctors have their own private clinics. You can also visit them there, but you have to wait if they are not available."

Acceptability

ACCEPTABILITY OF OUTPATIENT HEALTHCARE (SUPPLY SIDE)

One of the critical supply-side barriers associated with the acceptability aspect of healthcare access is the unwelcoming attitude or poor interpersonal skills of the healthcare providers (Paphassarang, Philavong, Boupha and Blas 2002). The interconnected issue in this case is the users' lack of trust in the healthcare providers or their intermediaries (Ozawa and Walker 2009). In order to highlight the barriers for people's reluctance in accessing health services, OPs were asked to rate their experiences during their most recent visit either to a healthcare provider or a facility selecting "very good", "good", "moderate", "poor" or "very poor". Acceptability is assessed with regard to the respondents' experiences of being treated respectfully, given clear explanations, being involved and feeling inclusive in decision-making, being talked to privately and provided access to a preferred or deemed better provider. As expected, once again, because of low reporting of "poor" or "very poor" experiences, these responses were combined with moderate ratings for purposes of analysis. On the different modes of acceptability, the highest percentage of OPs reported a "very good" experience at a private clinic, hospital or with a private doctor, followed by a primary healthcare centre, and lastly at the government hospital. One again, a high percentage of both high and poor ratings have been observed for the drugstores across the various levels of acceptability, making it difficult to assess a prevalent level of acceptability.

On whether OPs received respect from healthcare providers, many more OPs felt that they were treated with respect in the private healthcare facilities or doctors' offices (28 and 23 percent, respectively) in comparison to the primary healthcare centres (13 percent) or the government hospitals (9 percent). Only a very small proportion of the elderly visiting either a private or a government facility felt that the experience was less than good, i.e. "moderate", "poor" or "very poor" (Figure 6.11).

Pertaining to how clearly the healthcare providers explained things, only a small proportion of OPs had a "very good" experience at all the facilities, ranging from 13 percent at private clinics or hospitals, to 8 percent at the primary healthcare centres, i.e. *sub-RHCs* and RHCs, to a mere 1 percent at the government hospitals. At most facilities, fairly high percentages of OPs, from 33 to 37 percent, felt that their experience of healthcare providers was rated as "moderate" to "poor" in contrast to experiences at the private doctors' clinics wherein only 19 percent of respondents had a moderate to poor experience (Figure 6.12).

In relation to OP's experiences of being involved in decision-making about their treatment modalities, a much higher proportion of them felt that their experience was "very good" at either private clinics or hospitals (28 percent) or at private doctors' offices (22 percent), as compared to their experiences at government healthcare centres (0 percent). Only 7 percent of OPs visiting primary healthcare centres mentioned that they had had a "very good" experience with respect to decision-making. A higher percentage of OPs who sought

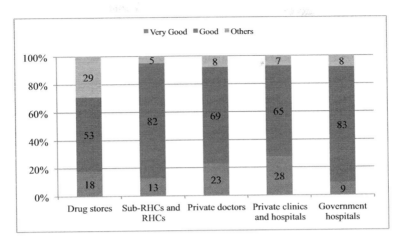

Figure 6.11 Perceptions of being treated respectfully by the healthcare provider or facility during most recent outpatient visit (percent distribution)

Source: Own calculations from the survey

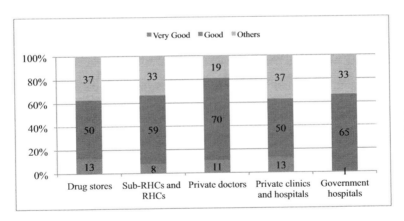

Figure 6.12 Perceptions of how clearly things were explained by the healthcare provider during the most recent outpatient visit (percent distribution)

Source: Own calculations from the survey

treatment at the drugstores and government-run facilities rated their experience of the decision-making process as "moderate to poor", compared to those who sought treatment at private facilities (Figure 6.13).

Once again, drugstores had the highest percentage of respondents reporting both "very good" and "moderate" to "very poor" in terms of their experience with regard to having an opportunity to speak privately with their care providers.

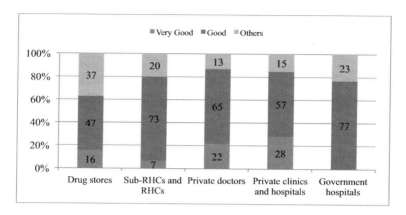

Figure 6.13 Perceptions of being involved in decision-making regarding treatment during the most recent outpatient visit (percent distribution)

Source: Own calculations from the survey

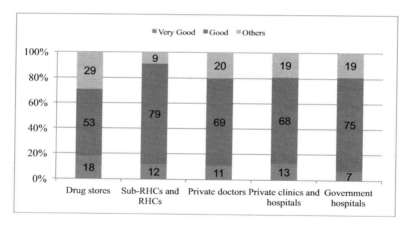

Figure 6.14 Perceptions of being provided an opportunity to speak privately with the healthcare provider during the most recent outpatient visit (percent distribution)

Source: Own calculations from the survey

Excluding drugstores, around 10 percent of those who accessed all the other health facilities felt that their experience with regard to having an opportunity to speak privately with their care providers was "very good". In contrast, about 20 percent felt that they had had a "moderate" or "very poor" experience at the various facilities, except at the PHCs, where only 9 percent had had a "moderate" to "very poor" experience (Figure 6.14). In addition, about one-third of respondents said that their access to a preferred healthcare provider was "moderate" to "very poor" across the gamut of healthcare facilities (Figure 6.15).

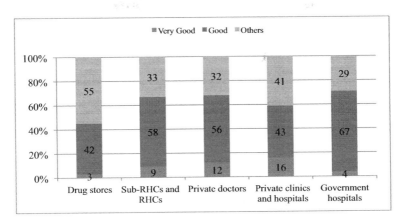

Figure 6.15 Perceptions regarding ease of access to a preferred provider at the facility during the most recent outpatient visit (percent distribution)

Source: Own calculations from the survey

ACCEPTABILITY OF INPATIENT HEALTHCARE (SUPPLY SIDE)

On the acceptability barriers to inpatient healthcare, OPs were enquired about their experiences during their most recent hospitalisation in connection to being treated respectfully, given clear explanations, included in decision-making, talked to privately, and given access to a preferred healthcare provider. They were asked to rate their experiences on a five-point scale, selecting "very good", "good", "moderate", "poor" and "very poor". As expected, once again because of low reporting as reflected in the responses "poor" and "very poor", these choices were combined with reports of "moderate" experiences for the purposes of analysis.

According to these different measures of acceptability, the highest percentage of OPs reported that their experiences at the private facilities were "good" or "very good". In contrast, the highest proportion of OPs reported "moderate", "poor" and "very poor" experiences at both the SRHCs and RHCs and government hospitals (Figure 6.16).

Nearly all of the OPs who were hospitalised in private hospitals thought that they had been treated respectfully and that medical issues had been explained to them clearly. About 15 percent of respondents who were hospitalised in district or general hospitals and 11 percent of those hospitalised in station or township hospitals reported experiences that were less than "good". Similarly, 23 percent of respondents hospitalised in district or general hospitals and 17 percent of those hospitalised in station or township hospitals reported that their experiences in relation to providers' explanations of medical matters were less than good (Figure 6.17 and Figure 6.18).

A high percentage of elderly persons reported that their experiences of being included in decision-making about treatment and having the opportunity to talk privately with healthcare providers were less than "good". A much lower

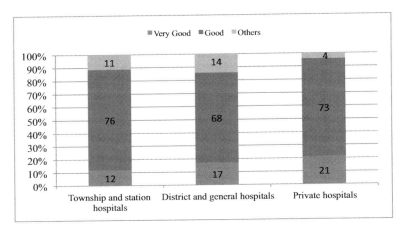

Figure 6.16 Perceptions of being treated respectfully by the healthcare provider or facility during the most recent hospitalisation (percent distribution)

Source: Own calculations from the survey

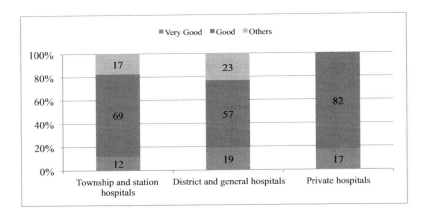

Figure 6.17 Perceptions of how clearly medical issues were explained by the health-care provider during the most recent hospitalisation (percent distribution)

Source: Own calculations from the survey

percentage of elderly persons hospitalised in private hospitals, however, reported a lack of involvement in decision-making about treatment modality (17 percent), in comparison to those hospitalised in government hospitals (36 to 38 percent).

Similarly, a much lower percentage of elderly people hospitalised in private hospitals reported a lack of opportunity to talk privately with healthcare

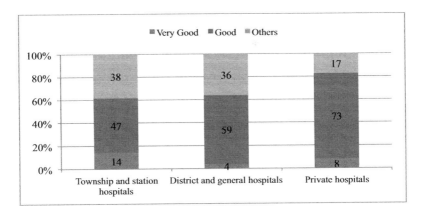

Figure 6.18 Perceptions of being involved in decision-making regarding treatment during the most recent hospitalisation (percent distribution)

Source: Own calculations from the survey

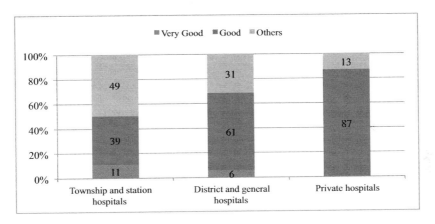

Figure 6.19 Perceptions of being provided an opportunity to speak privately with the healthcare provider during the most recent hospitalisation (percent distribution)

Source: Own calculations from the survey

providers (13 percent), in comparison to those who received services in government hospitals of different types (31 and 49 percent) (Figure 6.19).

Higher percentages of OPs who were hospitalised in different types of government hospitals reported that their access to preferred healthcare providers was less than "good" (19 to 25 percent), in comparison to those who were admitted to private hospitals (8 percent) (Figure 6.20). During the FGDs, OPs expressed corresponding remarks about government hospitals: "The doctors

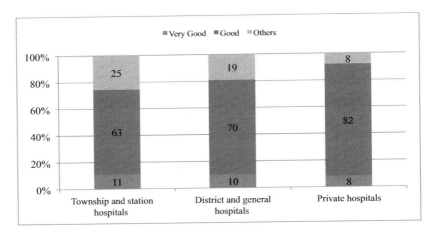

Figure 6.20 Perceptions regarding ease of access to a preferred provider at the facility during the most recent hospitalisation (percent distribution)

Source: Own calculations from the survey

and nurses are quite nice, but the auxiliary staff and workers are quite rude towards the patients' caregivers, shouting about insignificant errors all the time"; "There are really kind-hearted staff in the hospital, but unfortunately they are in the minority. As a result, many people do not notice these people and think arbitrarily that all the people in the hospital are bad".

6.5   Discussion and policy implications

It is true that midwives and other primary healthcare staff at the SRHCs are the first and sometimes the only trained healthcare providers that OPs in Myanmar are able to access. As previously noted, heavy reliance on midwives is less than ideal. However, since these personnel are already functioning as primary healthcare providers in many rural and remote areas, they should be provided opportunities for further training, requisite skill development and career enhancement.

Another profitable approach is to facilitate the inclusion of the Department of Traditional Medicine (DTM) in the entire comprehensive healthcare system. As an additional step, the DTM could train, certify, standardise and regulate the traditional medical practitioners scattered across the country to ensure that these practitioners become a valuable and reliable alternative source of healthcare, particularly in rural and remote areas. Furthermore, the DTM could act as a mechanism to regulate the manufacturing of traditional medicines. It is also commendable that easily accessible, dedicated geriatric clinics, similar to WHO-supported "Wednesday geriatrics clinics", established in the projected areas, are established widely to target OP's healthcare since as revealed during the FGDs, many OPs felt that they were not a priority group for government-run healthcare facilities as in the RHCs and various hospitals. The cost of private outpatient and particularly inpatient healthcare in Myanmar is forbiddingly higher compared with government healthcare. Although private healthcare has substantial affordability barriers, the ratings of user satisfaction with various healthcare services indicate a higher level of satisfaction with private healthcare compared to government healthcare facilities.

The availability and acceptability barriers associated with government healthcare facilities take the form of shortage of healthcare cadres, unqualified and underqualified healthcare cadres, lack of motivation among staff, lack of care and attention, disrespectful attitudes towards patients, lack of sanitation and hygiene, long waiting times and lack of availability of medications and other consumables. As noted by OPs in FGDs, the government healthcare facilities have improved over recent years. With the increased investment in recent years, there seems to be slow yet sure improvement. It implies that the government should try to increase investment in public healthcare significantly over the coming years, especially for infrastructure, human resources and increased remuneration for healthcare personnel.

6.6 Concluding remarks

The Myanmar healthcare system currently faces a myriad of challenges. The healthcare system, however, is not the sole responsibility of the Ministry of Health and Sports (MoHS). Many of the health inequities observed in this country are directly related to the social determinants of health, i.e. the conditions in which people are born, brought up, grow, live, work and age. These are mainly shaped by the distribution of money, power and resources. Actions from different sectors other than the healthcare sector are therefore equally, if not more, integral in improving national health and address systematic disparities. This requires close collaboration across various ministries and agencies. The major challenges facing the Myanmar healthcare system are lack of social health protection for the poor and elderly, low investment in rural health services, low level of government involvement in the health sector, transfer of financial burden of healthcare onto individual households and the incessant dependence on fluctuating and erratic foreign aid. In Myanmar, as in other low-income developing countries, access to adequate healthcare is inevitably linked to the larger questions of poverty, ethnic diversity, unstable political system and poor infrastructure development.

To achieve health equity and health rights in Myanmar, it is imperative that poverty needs to be tackled as a longer-term development objective. For the short term, group insurance programmes similar to the Rashtriya Swasthya Bima Yojana (RBBY) scheme in India could well be a way forward. Often occurring in poorer countries, the root cause of supply-side barriers to healthcare is the substantial gap that exists between actual health spending and the spending that is required to provide essential health services (WHO 2001; O'Donnell 2007). Similar conditions exist in Myanmar. In the goal towards expanding access and advancing health equity in the country, there is an urgent need to strengthen the existing healthcare system. Township-based rural healthcare facilities are currently one of the most accessible and affordable sources of healthcare, especially in rural areas, and thus the system should be enhanced through greater investment to expand its scope to reach greater numbers of poor, rural OPs.

References

Idler, E.L. and Y. Benyamini (1997) "Self-rated Health and Mortality: A Review of Twenty-seven Community Studies". *Journal of Health and Social Behaviour*, 38(1): 21–37.

Idler, E.L. and S.V. Kasl (1995) "Self-Ratings of Health: Do They Also Predict Change in Functional Ability?". *Journals of Gerontology: Social Sciences*, 50B: S344–S353.

Jacobs, B., Ir, P., Bigdeli, M., Annear, P.L. and W. Van Damme (2012) "Addressing Access Barriers to Health Services for the Poor: An Analytical Framework for Selecting Appropriate Interventions in Low Income Countries". *Health Policy and Planning*, 27(4): 288–300.

Khun, S. and L. Manderson (2007) "Health Seeking and Access to Care for Children With Suspected Dengue in Cambodia: An Ethnographic Study". *BMC Public Health*, 7: 262.

Kinsella, K. and W. He (2009) "An Aging World: 2008". U.S. Census Bureau, International Population Reports, P95/09–1, U.S. Government Printing Office.

Knodel, J. (2014) *The Situation of Older Persons in Myanmar: Results From the 2012 Survey of Older Persons* (Rev. 2014). Yangon: HelpAge International Myanmar Country Office (In Collaboration With HelpAge International Staff).

MoHS (2014) *Health in Myanmar 2014*. Nay Pyi Daw: Ministry of Health and Sports.

O'Donnell, O. (2007) "Access to Health Care in Developing Countries: Breaking Down Demand Side Barriers". *Cadernos de Saúde Pública*, 23: 2820–34.

Ozawa, S. and D.G. Walker (2009) "Trust in the Context of Community-based Health Insurance Schemes in Cambodia: Villagers' Trust in Health Insurers". *Advances in Health Economics and Health Services Research*, 21: 107–32.

Paphassarang, C., Philavong, K., Boupha, B. and E. Blas (2002) "Equity, Privatization and Cost Recovery in Urban Health Care: The Case of Lao PDR". *Health Policy and Planning*, 17(Supplement 1): 72–84.

Scommegna, P. (2012, August) "Noncommunicable Diseases Among Older Adults in Low- and Middle-Income Countries. Population Reference Bureau". *Today's Research on Aging*, 26.

Sreerupa and S.I. Rajan (2010) "Gender and Widowhood: Disparity in Health and Healthcare Utilization Among Aged in India". *Journal of Ethnic and Cultural Diversity in Social Work* (Special issue on Women and Aging International: Diversity, Challenges and Contributions), 19(4): 287–304.

Tandon, A., Murray, C.J.L., Lauer, J. and D. Evans (2000) *Measuring Overall Health System Performance for 191 Countries*. Geneva: World Health Organization (Global Program on Evidence for Health Policy Discussion Paper No. 30).

Teerawichitchainan, B. and J. Knodel (2015) "Economic Status and Old-age Health in Poverty-Stricken Myanmar". *Journal of Aging and Health*, 27(8): 1462–84.

Van Doorslaer, E., O'Donnell, O., Rannan-Eliya, R.P., Somanathan, A., Adhikari, S.R., Garg, C.C. . . . and A. Karan (2006) "Effect of Payments for Health Care on Poverty Estimates in 11 Countries in Asia: An Analysis of Household Survey Data". *The Lancet*, 368(9544): 1357–64.

World Health Organization (WHO) (2000) *The World Health Report 2000: Health Systems: Improving Performance*. Geneva: WHO.

————— (2001) *Commission on Macroeconomics and Health. Macroeconomics and Health: Investing in Health for Economic Development*. Geneva: WHO.

————— (2011a) *Global Status Report on Non-Communicable Diseases 2010*. Geneva: WHO.

————— (2011b) "Myanmar (Non-Communicable Diseases) Country Profiles 2011". URL: <www.who.int/nmh/countries/mmr_en.pdf> (accessed 6 May 2016).

————— (2014) "The Republic of the Union of Myanmar: Health System Review". *Health Systems in Transition (HiT)*, 4(3), WHO Press (on behalf of the Asia Pacific Observatory on Health Systems and Policies).

7 Policy options for protecting health rights of older people

Long Thanh Giang and Theresa W. Devasahayam

The country-specific analyses of the five ASEAN countries covered in this book, i.e. Singapore, Malaysia, Thailand, Vietnam and Myanmar, has shown that there are vast differences between countries in protecting health rights for older people, mostly because of differences in socioeconomic and health systems development. The healthcare systems in these five countries are substantially different in terms of key performance indicators such as life expectancy, total health expenditure as a percent of GDP and out-of-pocket payment as a percent of the total health expenditure. At the same time, thorough analyses for all studied countries indicated a variety of shortcomings in protecting the health of older persons (OPs) in terms of accessibility, acceptability, affordability and satisfaction with healthcare services. Overall, all country chapters confirm various imperatives in reforming healthcare systems in order to protect the health rights of OPs. The key driver for swift action is rapid population ageing in all the selected countries in this study. Except for Singapore and Malaysia, the other three countries at lower levels of income have witnessed a rapid increase in the share of OPs in the total population, and the scenario of "getting old before getting rich" is quite clear. Such a situation in turn requires greater effort from governments and their citizens to meet the healthcare needs of OPs in the coming years.

Comprehensive and well-functioning healthcare systems are urgently needed for protecting the health rights of citizens in general, and OPs in particular. A robust healthcare system not only provides accessible, adequate and affordable services to the older generation, but also to future cohorts of OPs (i.e., the current younger generations). Because the healthcare needs in the various countries selected for study differ, the common health issues among OPs (such as NCDs, disability and immobility) mean that a number of policies and programmes with a long-term vision and strategy must be in place. Healthcare policies and programmes alone will not be able to help OPs to attain "healthy ageing", rather, comprehensive and mutually supportive policies and programmes should be put in place to ensure that the numerous socioeconomic and health challenges faced by OPs today as a result of a demographic shift can be met.

In the following sections, policy options to protect the health rights of OPs in each country, followed by ASEAN-wide policy implications, are provided.

7.1 Country-specific policy options

7.1.1 *Singapore*

In spite of being the most affluent country among the ASEAN member states, its elderly population remains a vulnerable group. Studies have found that they are less healthy and have fewer savings than their younger counterparts. In response to a growing ageing population, and cognizant that large pockets among them may have difficulties undertaking healthcare expenses, the government has taken significant steps in the last few years to meet the health needs of OPs. Generally, OPs have responded positively to these schemes, although much more can be done to empower them in terms of their overall health rights. The following are policies and actions that the government should consider to meet the health needs of its ageing population:

1   *For the whole of society:* ageing policies should adopt the rights approach with the aim of empowering and enabling OPs to access appropriate and affordable healthcare more independently and by not overly relying on family or the community. Socioeconomic development strategies and policies should aim to integrate OPs into the labour force and other productive activities so as to enable OPs to keep up with the rising costs of healthcare and to encourage active ageing.

2   *For the provision of healthcare services:* ensure quality healthcare for greater numbers of OPs irrespective of affordability on the part of the individual since there is a lingering perception that the quality of health services is uneven depending on affordability. In this regard, there should be mechanisms in place to ensure that patients are not receiving poorer or insufficient healthcare depending on the type of ward to which one is admitted. Structural mechanisms should be put in place to enable and empower the elderly so that they able to make appropriate choices for themselves in terms of accessing relevant health and social care since currently the choices they have tend to be circumscribed by the twin factors of affordability, on the one hand, and a heavy dependence on next-of-kin or the community, on the other.

3   *For healthcare financing:* aim at reducing health inequalities across the different socioeconomic groups among OPs. There should be consideration given to creating a finance mechanism to ensure that outpatient health services available at public health facilities outside office hours and during weekends should be affordable to all OPs in keeping with the notion of "affordable healthcare for all". Subsidies should apply to such services and not impose fees that are prohibitive especially for OPs from the lower socioeconomic groups. Consideration should be given to creating a mechanism to ensure that OPs stricken with cancer will have access to timely and relevant health services. A finance mechanism needs to be in place to ensure that those in the lower socioeconomic group will have access to heavy

subsidies and that any incurred healthcare expenses are not shifted to their next-of-kin who may already be facing financial difficulties.

4   *For educating older people*: strengthen information and education communication (IEC) so as to empower OPs. In this regard, the government should raise the knowledge levels of OPs in regard to their eligibility to access the different existing health schemes as well as maintaining a healthy lifestyle. While the majority are aware of the most recent health schemes rolled out for OPs and understand that these schemes significantly reduce out-of-pocket payment on their part particularly when visiting public health facilities, knowledge on exactly how each scheme has benefitted OPs is largely thin. Reaching out to the lower socioeconomic groups is paramount, especially since those who had poorer health outcomes and from the lower socioeconomic groups seemed to have lower levels of health education.

7.1.2 Malaysia

1   *For the provision of healthcare services*: close the gap in healthcare services in rural and urban areas. Specialist services will need to be developed and made more easily available in the rural areas. OPs from rural and indigenous minorities should be provided with healthcare services which are affordable, accessible, and culturally acceptable in line with the National Health Policy for Older persons 2008. Health services should also provide a holistic system of care of OPs through the further development of generic services as well as urgent policy responses in terms of specialist services including psycho-geriatric care demand to meet the growing needs of an ageing population. Priority should be given to providing a spectrum of care services from home assistance to those who are dependent, as well as care for acute and chronic illnesses. Mental health issues such as dementia and depression among OPs are emerging and require interventions from all medical personnel, including social workers.

2   *For human resource development in healthcare for OPs*: raise geriatric competency among healthcare personnel through curricula training targeted at different levels of healthcare providers. Aside from equipping health officials with knowledge on geriatric medicine, it is also critical to ensure that their knowledge of the psychology of ageing, and skills on interpersonal relationship building are strengthened. Ageism among healthcare providers need to be addressed.

3   *For reviewing and evaluating the need of OPs on a periodic basis*: review current policies and programmes to evaluate their effectiveness in meeting the healthcare needs of OPs. The Malaysian Research Institute of Ageing could be tasked to carry out the review and provide feedback to the government on elderly policies and programmes and the extent to which the needs of OPs have been met.

4   *For more effective provision of income security*: strengthen income security for OPs since health and income security are closely associated. Current

support schemes are means-tested and were found to be inadequate to support the health needs of OPs. Universal access to healthcare insurance, to include long-term care and disability payment (EFP, SOCSO [Social security organisation], Private).

7.1.3 *Thailand*

All OPs in Thailand are protected by some form of universal coverage, but the quality of care is still a concern. The following is a list of policy options to strengthen the health needs of OPs:

1 *For the provision of healthcare services:* improve community-based long-term care (LTC). Coordination mechanisms should be strengthened to ensure that community-based models of LTC implemented at the local level. There should be health promotion activities for OPs.
2 *For human resource development in healthcare for OPs:* strengthen human resources to implement the community-based LTC models. There should be consideration of scaling up the models as well as the services linked to them, as well as ensuring their coverage and funding their sustainability.
3 *For achieving a healthy lifestyle:* support "active ageing" of OPs at district and community levels. There should be relevant policies and interventions to encourage active ageing among OPs and the impact of these policies and interventions should be evaluated. There should also be health preventive interventions directed at reducing the burden of diseases especially non-communicable diseases (NCDs) across the different age cohorts so that future generations of OPs have fewer morbidities and disabilities in old age.

7.1.4 *Vietnam*

There is a great demand for promoting appropriate responses to health problems associated with population ageing. The following are priorities that Vietnam must pursue in the coming years:

1 *For the whole of society:* raise awareness of the needs of older persons and caregivers for OPs to successfully achieve healthy ageing. Population ageing must be taken into account in developing socioeconomic development strategies and policies (UNFPA 2011).
2 *For achieving a healthy lifestyle:* create models for meeting chronic disease management of older persons in the community. The government should also ensure continuity of care with models that are appropriate for different environments and increase awareness and knowledge of OPs and families about how to maintain and improve the health of OPs. There should be programmes to facilitate health promotion through exercise, diet, smoking cessation or other public health interventions aimed at OPs. There should be an increase in occupational and physical therapy or other interventions

to increase physical functioning and maintaining independence for OPs as their health deteriorates or after they face health problems such as hospitalisation or injury after falling (MOH and Health Partnership Group 2017).

3 *For the provision of healthcare services:* ensure that caregivers, social workers and health workers are adequately trained and supervised to deal with the specific needs of older persons. There should be the setting up of a system to record and report on healthcare for OPs. There should be mechanisms to strengthen the system of routine and ad-hoc (internal and external) monitoring, supervision and evaluation of the performance of healthcare for OPs at all levels. There should be efforts to carry out periodic surveys on older persons to monitor and supervise the implementation of activities and output indicators in healthcare and other areas; strengthen IEC on healthcare for OPs through appropriate channels with contents suitable with the needs for disease prevention, health promotion for OPs, early detection of diseases and palliative care. There should be programmes to provide older people information about health facilities capable of examining, treating or managing their diseases. The government should promote collaboration among the health sector and other line ministries and organisations involved in health promotion for OPs and to strengthen the functions of commune health centres in medical examination and management of chronic diseases (MOH and Health Partnership Group 2017).

4 *For healthcare financing:* promote and reach the goal of universal health insurance coverage by considering subsidy policy for health insurance and encouraging family members and social organisations to buy health insurance so that all older persons are covered. In addition, cost effectiveness analyses for health insurance-paid healthcare packages for OPs should be taken into account under limited resources. A special financing mechanism to services provided to disabled and vulnerable groups of OPs so as to increase their access to adequate services should be considered. In addition, consideration should be given to provide incentives and accountability in the delivery of healthcare to OPs at the commune level so that commune health workers will be more active in managing and providing care to OPs (MOH and Health and Finance Governance 2016; Giang, Pham and Pham 2016).

5 *For human resource development in healthcare for OPs:* develop geriatrics competencies as the basis for modifying the training of general doctors, specialists related to older persons and nurses caring for elderly patient. There should be a review, update, revision and amendment of undergraduate, junior college and secondary training curricula in the health sciences towards meeting the healthcare needs of older persons. The government should aim to provide continuous training in geriatrics for health workers involved in medical care for OPs with greater emphasis placed on contents of health counselling for OPs so that they can take care of themselves, improve their health and provide advice on end-of-life palliative care. Moreover, there should be the strengthening of the network and capacity related to geriatric care (MOH and Health Partnership Group 2017).

7.1.5 *Myanmar*

Legal instruments and constitutional documents such as the 2008 Constitution show in different ways how the country is moving forward towards protecting the right to healthcare: "Every citizen shall, in accord with the health policy laid down by the Union, have the right to health care". The Law Relating to Older Persons was recently promulgated in December 2016, and one of the aims is to "include easily accessible health services for the elderly people in the National Health Care Schemes". The law stands in need of health systems to "arrange for the elderly people to obtain well-qualified, appropriate medical treatments in readily accessible places either free or at reduced rates," along with affordable medication. The law also guarantees OPs the "right to obtain with dignity the supports from family care, home-based, community-based care in their own community".

The National Health Plan 2017–2021 makes a strong commitment to pro-poor Universal Health Coverage (UHC), which cannot be reached without addressing the needs of an ageing population and the rising rates of non-communicable diseases (NCDs) and disability. Myanmar is also committed to international declarations and agreements such as MIPAA (Madrid International Plan of Action on Ageing) and the Kuala Lumpur Declaration on Ageing (2015) in order to maintain universal and equal access to healthcare service and the provision of a continuum of care and services for older people. Thus, Myanmar has a sufficient amount of enabling conditions in terms of policy-level legislation, but there has been fewer actions taken suggesting that implementation tends to be weak because of the many constraints and challenges that have emerged at all levels. In this respect, consideration should be given to prioritise healthcare and rights to access healthcare at the implementation level among older citizens.

1 *For achieving a healthy lifestyle:* widespread replication of OPs' associations (in Myanmar, Older People's Self-Help Groups) in order to maintain functional ability and general well-being of OPs in an active and healthy society. The government should also consider introducing nationwide elderly physical exercise programmes and clubs with special guidance and support of the Ministry of Health and Sport.
2 *For the provision of healthcare services:* install and upgrade geriatric units in all government hospitals, improve government hospitals' facilities with free-of-charge services to all OPs. The government should ensure well-functioning and accessible weekly geriatric clinics at all village tracts and ward levels with sufficient essential drugs. There should also be the inclusion of a Department of Traditional Medicine in the healthcare system and that the treatment, care and support available under the department should be evidence-based, scientific and reliable. The government should set up regular monitoring and evaluation systems within the healthcare system to keep abreast of any developments in programmes related to elderly healthcare on both the supply and demand sides. The government

should establish efficient inter-ministerial cooperation taking a whole-of-government (WOG) approach in addressing the health needs of OPs in order to provide collective and synergetic effort in drafting a National Plan of Action on Ageing with strong recommendations of elderly healthcare components by incorporating elements from existing ministerial plans and policies.

3 *For healthcare financing:* introduce a basic health insurance programme specifically for OPs and a provision of universal social pension with lower age ceiling.

4 *For human resource development in healthcare for OPs:* expand network of basic healthcare coverage and increase basic health staff (e.g. midwife, health assistant, public health supervisor, etc.) down to the grassroots levels, especially in rural and remote areas. There should be consideration given to providing continuous medical education, regular TOT (training of trainers) and refresher training, skill development and career enhancement programmes for healthcare personnel. There is also a need to improve knowledge and skills in geriatric healthcare by introducing customised curriculum of geriatric care to different levels among healthcare staff and encouraging them to pursue geriatric medicine and gerontology for future careers. There should also be the provision of on-job training and effective teaching programmes in terms of geriatric medicine for undergraduate, post graduate and doctorate levels.

5 *For educating the elderly:* design and conduct public health awareness programmes for OPs, including advocacy programmes for key stakeholders. There should be efforts to increase media coverage and outreach of health and care awareness raising programmes for OPs and their families.

6 *For data collection on ageing trends:* broaden the research work relating to healthcare, rights, demographic changes and its implications, as well as conduct a national health survey for OPs. The government should ensure the collection of reliable data and statistics in all aspects of elderly healthcare and maintain a national-level database system such as an evidence-based follow-up system.

7.2 ASEAN-wide priorities for protecting health rights of older people

It should be taken for granted that different countries will have different priorities in healthcare system reforms in order to protect the health rights of their respective older populations, given the wide disparity in socioeconomic development levels and the existing healthcare systems across the five ASEAN countries. At the same time, a variety of common health issues have emerged in the ageing populations of the five countries which means that specific healthcare system reforms need to be put in place. In this section, we outline key ASEAN-wide themes in healthcare reforms which might be critical to protect the health rights for older populations.

7.2.1 Build up a national plan for protecting health rights of older people

Currently, all ASEAN countries have healthcare policies and programmes for OPs, but they are quite fragmented, especially in low- and middle-income countries. In order to have an integrated and comprehensive healthcare system for citizens in general, and OPs in particular, there is a great need to build up a strategic national plan for an old-age healthcare system, in which its specific plans should have clear visions and actions to deal with the growing needs of care resulting from the increasing number of OPs. The visions and actions should consider various country-specific factors resulting from the pathways of socioeconomic growth and development along with a consideration of the possible health issues that emerge as a result of population ageing.

7.2.2 Build a national consensus on ageing and related issues, including health and long-term care, through evidence-based policy dialogues

Among the most important policy concerns relevant to ageing and ageing-related issues are the future viability of social protection schemes, including those for health and long-term care services provided to OPs. In designing policies and programmes, policymakers should need to know, for example, the health issues of OPs in tangent with several key questions: (a) how physically and mentally capable are older people? (b) what is the trajectory of health and function as people age? (c) how can healthcare services be provided in such a manner as to maintain optimal health and function? and, (d) how much should be invested in transforming the healthcare system (including the inclusion of new technologies, improved service delivery and upskilling of human resources)? Through constant dialogues between policymakers and relevant stakeholders on different aspects of population ageing and related strategies and policies for OPs, a national consensus can be built, and this in turn would contribute to establishing a national plan for protecting the health rights for older people.

7.2.3 Promote equity in healthcare services among older people

It is clear from the studied countries that, regardless of how sophisticated, modern and comprehensive health services might be in a country, accessibility and utilisation of healthcare services of OPs are uneven by such important factors as socioeconomic status, ethnicity and geographic location. Such inequity in healthcare services might be a result of various factors related to older individuals (demand side), and from the variation within the health system in terms of quality of care (supply side). These factors highlight efforts of governments in transforming policies and programmes on healthcare in order to promote equity among OPs in receiving healthcare services.

7.2.4   *Achieve adequate and affordable healthcare services for older people*

In some low- and low-middle-income countries in ASEAN, a large proportion of the older population are not covered by a social health insurance (SHI) system. This is reflected by the fact that older people and their families must bear huge out-of-pocket payments for the received healthcare services, which in turn could impoverish them. Moreover, regardless of having SHI or not, older people sometimes do not get adequate healthcare services, in which the most common examples include misapplication of therapies and overuse of medications and devices. Inadequate and/or unaffordable healthcare services result in OPs, particularly the poor and the vulnerable, becoming marginalised because of poor health. In order to achieve adequate and affordable healthcare services for OPs, along with transforming healthcare services, SHI schemes should also be reformed so as to ensure financial sustainability of the healthcare system, as well as reduce out-of-pocket burden.

7.2.5   *Build up national data, including health-related indicators, on ageing and older people*

Diverse data and information used in the analyses of health rights for older people in the five studied countries have indicated that there has been a significant shortage of national data on ageing and OPs, and in particular their health rights. Some countries, on the one hand, have nationally-representative data on older people but they are not collected regularly, and different national surveys could produce different results for the same indicators because of differences in sampling methods and specific foci. On the other hand, some countries do not have national surveys on OPs, and all analyses must be based on small-scaled and unrepresentative data. These issues have prevented producing reliable/quality evidence-based studies for policymaking. Thus, the building up of national data, including health-related indicators, on ageing and older people are critical, especially to generate evidence-informed policies.

References

Giang, T.L., Pham, T.H.T. and L.T. Pham (2016) "Bao hiem y te trong cham soc suc khoe nguoi cao tuoi o Vietnam" (Social Health Insurance in Health Care for Older People in Vietnam). *Journal of Economics & Development*, 231(II): 38–48.

MOH and Health and Finance Governance (HFG) (2016) *Actuarial Analysis of Healthcare Services Paid by Social Health Insurance in Vietnam*. Hanoi: MOH & HFG.

MOH and Health Partnership Group (2017) *Joint Annual Health Report (JARH) 2016: Towards a Healthy Ageing*. Hanoi: MOH.

UNFPA (United Nations Population Fund) (2011) *The Aging Population in Vietnam: Current Status, Prognosis, and Possible Policy Responses*. Hanoi: UNFPA.

8 Conclusions

Theresa W. Devasahayam and Long Thanh Giang

The majority of ASEAN countries are ageing at a much faster rate than their developed counterparts that are at a similar stage of demographic transition. It could be said that a rapid demographic transition is indicative of the "success that developing countries have had in improving the welfare of their populations" as a result of installing relevant policies to boost the welfare and well-being of their citizenry (Barrientos 2010: 587). While many of the ASEAN countries are expected to continue to surge forward in the years to come supported by robust domestic demand – a critical driver of growth in these countries (International Monetary Fund 2017) – as well as trade liberalisation and worker mobility, this suggests that a rapidly ageing population could be a potential setback for countries as more resources have to be channelled into meeting the needs of the older population in respect to healthcare and income security coupled with lower labour force participation and savings rates (Bloom, Canning and Fink 2010).

It has been found that over the recent years, the ASEAN countries have a higher than average proportion of working age adults, or what is called the demographic dividend, from its young, expanding workforce – a trend that will remain until 2030. In fact, estimates have it that the working age population in ASEAN will account for 68 percent of the region's total population by 2025 (Iskyan 2016). What this means is that these countries have a greater share of workers who then save and pay taxes, which benefits the economy since there is an increase in growth in income levels. Because of the demographic dividend coupled with strong growth policies, there have been assertions made that there is reason to be optimistic in terms of the region's economic growth, of which it can boast of a combined gross domestic product (GDP) of about $2.6 trillion, making it collectively the third largest economy in Asia and the seventh largest in the world (Asian Development Bank 2017), in spite of countries in the region experiencing population ageing (Iskyan 2016). In this case, there are effects of population ageing on the development of countries albeit these are influenced by policy choices and the health and functional status of older persons (OPs) (cf. Lloyd-Sherlock 2010). In Singapore for example, while immigration can soften the blow of an ageing population and declining fertility rates, stop-gap measures might not prove to be viable in the long run given that skilled immigrants in the destination country could always turn to 'greener pastures'.

In order for countries in the ASEAN region to continue to attain continuous economic growth and a satisfactory GDP, the strategies of these countries would have to shift. Well-targeted structural reforms are needed to boost productivity and stir economic growth. These can be achieved through the reallocation of labour from the low productivity sectors such as agriculture to the higher productivity sectors such as industry and service sectors (Bloom, Canning and Fink 2010). Other ways of spurring economic growth rates are to focus on technological progress, human capital, institutions and governance, macroeconomic and trade policies and random shocks.

The reforms should also aim towards generating inclusive policies aimed at OPs such as retaining older workers in the labour force and capitalising on their skills, expertise and experience (Zaidi 2015). In this regard, OPs should be ensured opportunities to participate actively in the labour force and receive a share of the development benefits reaped by the country. Doing so would also suggest that OPs are viewed as an asset in the development plan of countries and are not seen as a "waste of a resource", since this group has enormous value to the economy (Randal, German and Ewing 1999). In turn, relaxing the retirement age requirements to enable OPs to actively engage in the workforce is also imperative.

Recognising the rights of OPs is also crucial to being inclusive and the merits of inclusivity cannot be underestimated since it engenders social cohesion. In spite of the strong economic record of the majority of countries in the ASEAN region, the basic rights of OPs have been found to be largely unrecognised. OPs continue to face discrimination in the labour force and in terms of receiving old age support and care – all of which have a bearing on the experiences of growing old. Moreover, OPs' rights to affordable, accessible and appropriate health services have also been denied. The denial of the health rights of OPs is bound up with a confluence of factors ranging from the kind of elderly policies formulated in the respective countries to structural and infrastructural impediments. In light of this, securing the health rights of OPs is especially critical since there is no denying that health is an integral factor for active ageing. In this regard, putting in place relevant policies, measures and programmes become ever more important in securing the health rights of the old age cohort in the population.

Protecting the health rights of OPs goes a long way in contributing towards the development of the country since it presents the opportunity for tapping into the human capital of this group. This can be achieved through relevant and appropriate social and economic policies supporting OPs' employment, income, health and autonomy. In fact, the Sustainable Development Goals (SDGs) recognise the role of OPs for sustainable development as encapsulated in Goal 3: ensure healthy lives and promote well-being for all at all ages (Zaidi 2015).

Given this, the diversity of national trajectories of economic and social development has the effect of shaping the ageing experience, as asserted by Lloyd-Sherlock (2010); to put it another way, people's experiences of old age would depend on the developmental stage of a country. The converse also holds true: population ageing has the potential of affecting how development strategies of countries are designed.

Whether countries are characterised as high- or low-income depending on the developmental stage they may be at, the approach to managing the health rights of their people would be very different. Higher income countries such as Singapore and Malaysia have an easier task before them since they only have to deal with chronic illnesses and other illnesses associated with old age, such as dementia and Alzheimer's disease. In contrast, low- and middle-income countries such as Thailand, Vietnam and Myanmar have to battle both infectious diseases and chronic illnesses. As Shetty (2012: 1285) puts it, for them, "longevity comes with a cruel twist". Thus, the problems of ageing are compounded for low-income countries in terms of ensuring adequate, appropriate and relevant healthcare.

In light of this, that which is critical is the question of whether developing countries are able to attain decent levels of economic growth to spur these countries into the next stage of development in spite of its rapid ageing population as well as meet the needs of an ageing population. And to this, the strategies policymakers adopt will determine the extent to which they are able to cope with their ageing populations and decide if the health rights of their older citizens are worth protecting.

References

Asian Development Bank (2017) "The Association of Southeast Asian Nations (ASEAN): 12 Things to Know". 8 November. URL: <www.adb.org/features/asean-12-things-know> (accessed 9 January 2018).

Barrientos, Armando (2010) "Population Ageing and International Development: From Generalisation to Evidence (Review)". *Canadian Journal on Aging/La Revue canadienne du vieillissement*, 29(4): 587–8.

Bloom, David E., Canning, David and Günther Fink (2010) "Implications of Population Ageing for Economic Growth". *Oxford Review of Economic Policy*, 26(4): 583–612.

International Monetary Fund (2017) "Asia's Dynamic Economies Continue to Lead Global Growth". URL: <www.imf.org/en/News/Articles/2017/05/08/NA050917-Asia-Dynamic-Economies-Continue-to-Lead-Global-Growth> (accessed 9 January 2018).

Iskyan, Kim (2016) "How this 'Dividend' Is Transforming ASEAN". Stansberry Churchouse Research, 9 November. URL: <http://stansberrychurchouse.com/china/how-this-dividend-is-transforming-asean/> (accessed 9 January 2018).

Lloyd-Sherlock, Peter (2010) *Population Ageing and International Development: From Generalisation to Evidence.* Bristol: Policy Press.

Randal, Judith, German, Tony and Deborah Ewing (eds.) (1999) *The Ageing & Development Report: Poverty, Independence and the World's Older People*. UK: HelpAge International and Earthscan.

Shetty, Priya (2012) "Grey Matter: Ageing in Developing Countries". *The Lancet*, 379(9823): 1285–7.

Zaidi, Asghar (2015) "Ageing and Development". United Nations Development Programme, 13 November. URL: <http://hdr.undp.org/en/content/ageing-and-development> (accessed 9 January 2018).

Index